Images of the West:
portraits in diversity —

WHAT ARE YOUR CHOICES?

BY

GEORGE A. FARRAH

First Printing

Sunray Publishing
25123 22nd Avenue
St. Cloud, MN 56301

Manufactured in the United States of America

ISBN-10: 1-934478-00-8
ISBN-13: 978-1-934478-00-4

To my son

George Joseph Farrah

for his continued interest

and for encouraging me

to write this book.

FOREWORD

We are at a crossroads in American history as we face some of the more serious challenges that we have ever faced in the past. A new millennium is before us and it is only through transformational leadership practiced at every level in our organizations, companies and government will we best able to regain the cultural vitality that we once had as a nation. Anyone familiar with the workplace knows that a unique type of leadership can impact and bring about the needed changes in any organization. Transformational leadership focuses on values, purity of purpose and service to others. It is really akin to the Stephen Covey's 7 Habits of Highly Effective People – leaders and individuals working together for the "good of the whole" while both recognizing differences as well as celebrating them.

This book, the result of a lifetime of research and study, examines the forces shaping American life and individuals' quest for meaning and identity in the 21st century. Dr. Farrah helps the reader think about those forces shaping us everyday in a new and different way. Subtly, he challenges us to become part of the solution through awareness of the nine values of acculturation and the true practice of the Golden Rule.

Lastly, this book serves as a clarion call to each of us and the organizations we work for to re-examine our motives and look for ways to affirm one another and to find a cure for the spiritual glaucoma, i.e., loss of heart and soul, we see so often manifested around us. The choice is ours – what will we do to positively impact our society, our families and our fellow citizens? In other words, what will be our legacy?

Read this book for new and unique insights into the forces which have shaped American life as we now know it. Dr. Farrah has done a great service to our country by laying these issues and trends before us. They are too significant for our future as a great nation to be ignored.

Dr. Robert C. Cavanna
Resource Traning and Solutions
Executive Director and
Chief Executive Officer
St. Cloud, Minnesota

ACKNOWLEDGMENTS

This book was made possible by the cooperative, dedicated efforts, and diverse talents of individuals here, at St. Cloud State University (SCSU), elsewhere in Minnesota, and Europe—particularly in Germany, Spain, and Switzerland. Some idea of the magnitude regarding the work and time involved can be gained via the numerous individuals who helped me and noting the kinds of services they rendered. Accordingly, I express my profound gratitude to these persons, here, in our country or those located elsewhere for their input and contributions.

I am deeply grateful to Randal Kolb, Director Emeritus of the center for Computing and Technology Services and my personal friend of long standing. It was he who processed the data resulting from the four SCSU funded research projects which I received over the years when I was actively involved at the university. In addition to these funded projects, utilizing his computer expertise, Randy assisted me in processing over three hundred graduate students' field studies—beyond the Master's degree and at the Specialist level. His suggestions for using various designs or models of statistics—from the analysis of variance to factor analysis—were successfully transferred into the language of the computer.

Others at the university assisted me with their valuable suggestions and insights regarding various phases or aspects of my research. In effect, my colleagues were intent on ensuring a logical sequence and integration of ideas for the various chapters or sections of my book. Therefore, for their gracious willingness to assist me with their helpful suggestions, time, and effort, I express my thanks to Dr. John W. Palmer, Professor of Health, Physical Education, Recreation, and Sport Sciences; Dr. James B. Anderson, Professor of English; Dr. Ruth K. Meyer, Professor and Vice-President Emeritus, Academic Affairs; and Dr. Leslie R. Green, Director, Office of Diversity, College of Education. I am profoundly grateful and express my thanks to Dr. Alfred A. Pabst, Professor Emeritus of Management and Finance at SCSU. Not only was Al extremely helpful in sharing his ideas and wisdom, but he constantly encouraged me to continue my work on values in America and Europe. Al and his wife Astrid have been a source of inspiration to me and remain my dearest of friends over all these years.

In the section of my book relating to the very important topic of "The Challenges to Farming and the Rural Way of Life," four individuals, who are knowledgeable with practical experiences in farming or rural living, were of considerable help to me. Consequently, my recognition and thanks are due to Mr. Darol Melby, who before his retirement, worked for the U.S. Department of Agriculture and the U.S. Conservation Services; Mr. Albert Toriseva, Superintendent Emeritus, Bagley Public Schools, and former part-time farmer; and Mr. James Martin, a retired elementary teacher and administrator who grew up on a farm. These three men remain my friends of thirty years, and they still reside in the Bagley, MN area. In addition, Mr. Bob Lefebre, Executive Director of the MN Milk Producers Association, also granted me an in-depth interview. I thank Bob for sharing his ideas concerning the American dairy farmer.

I would be remiss not to describe the tremendous impact, encouragement, and support which was given to me by the leadership and staff of Resource, Training, and Solutions (R.T., and S). As an influential organization within the St. Cloud Metropolitan Region, and being in the network of several, regional Minnesota Service Cooperatives, it currently serves forty-one school districts across Central Minnesota. Not only does R.T. and S. provide a number of educational services to both public and Catholic schools in this region, but it also offers and conducts extremely useful workshops, seminars, or consultant services for many businesses or social organizations for improving the infrastructure of St. Cloud. In terms of its glowing record of achievements, it deserves far more recognition and acclaim than it currently receives. I know these aforesaid facts from personal experiences!

For example, since my "retirement" (really a misnomer in my case!) from SCSU, and beginning during the year of 1988, I volunteered my services to R.T. and S. My first role consisted of being the Director of the Center for the American Way of Life (AWOL); and, then, during 1995, I became Director of the Center for the Study of Values—another voluntary position that I continue to serve to the present.

During the aforesaid time interval, Dr. Robert (Rob) C. Cavanna, the Chief Executive Officer of R.T. and S., has been a dynamic catalyst for innovating several of my projects in his region as well as elsewhere. Many school districts from Benson to Belgrade, to Chatfield or Chosen Valley, and to Bagley—all in Minnesota—participated in several of my workshops for teachers and parents. Most important, throughout my eighteen years of association with R.T. and S., Rob and his dedicated, cooperative staff have provided their diverse talents and skills to several outstanding research projects. Within the school district that was involved at the time, the research was adapted to formats featuring themes and topics such as: Improving Academic Self-concept and Motivation for Students and Teachers; Treatment Models for Effective Cross-Cultural and Gender-Fair Education; and Nine Values of Acculturation of Helping Youth Cope, Interact, and Apply Their Skills.

One such seminar, as a prototype of the many that were conducted at Resource, Training, and Solutions in their spacious St. Cloud location and elsewhere, the September 12th, 1990 seminar was outstanding. Held at the Holiday Inn of Bemidji, Minnesota it was a cooperative effort arranged by Dr. Cavanna and Ms. Kristen Woodcock, then the Special Projects Coordinator for the Northwest Minnesota Educational Cooperative Service Unit in Thief River Falls. Its main purpose, involving teachers, administrators, and a state senator, was to create a school and community climate for cross-cultural education. Therefore, for his continued support and loyalty, I express my deepest appreciation to my colleague and friend who is less formally known as "Rob."

In terms of my research in Europe, the trip I took to Madrid, Spain was most productive. My many thanks and gratitude are given to Sister Renee Domeier, O.S.B., Ph.D., and Professor Emeritus, St. Benedict College, for inviting me to her Study Center during 1982; to Mr. Augusto Cucala, Castellan, Spain, for administering my questionnaire (i.e., a Spanish version of AWOL); and to Professor Joaquin Fabregat, University of Madrid, for sharing his ideas and suggestions.

Others in Europe were also helpful over the years. I am grateful to Mr. Martin Bizer who as a teacher, brought groups of his German high school students on a yearly basis, during the 1990's, to Lindstrom (MN) High School to interact with students and members of the community. Concurrent during his stay, I often visited his groups in order to interact with his students regarding cross-cultural issues. Then during September,

2004, Martin invited me to visit the Wirtemberg-Gymnasium, not far from Korb, Germany, where he is now the director. While there, I team taught an eleventh grade class concerning the various categories of AWOL. It was with Lars Koehler, an inspirational teacher to whom I again, more formally express my thanks for this unique opportunity in enhancing cross-cultural education through cooperative team teaching—in both German and English!

Then, while in Switzerland, I interviewed the Director of the Transportation Museum. Later I visited my long-time friends, Mr. and Mrs. George and Christine Huegli of Baden, Rutihof, which is near Zurich. As a teacher in the "Primar und Sekundasschule" (i.e., Primary and Secondary School) at Gebenstorf, Aargau, Switzerland, she teaches children of families who have emigrated from 21 countries of the world—from Albania to Zimbabwe! Over the years, in my frequent visits to see them, we have shared ideas regarding cross-cultural education as well as AWOL. Then, following a suggestion I made to Christine during my visit in 2004, Christie organized a program where she and other colleagues are teaching German to the mothers from the many countries noted above. Her innovation was highly successful for the mothers and children in adjusting to the acculturation process in Switzerland. For their significant and splendid contributions, Christine and her colleagues were featured in three regional newspapers during June, July, and August of 2005. Moreover, with their interest and awareness of my involvement in cross-cultural education, they exposed me to the art, literature and music of their area in particular and to Switzerland in general. For these wonderful learning experiences, I am grateful to them.

Much closer to home, I thank my son, George Joseph and my granddaughter, Kaelie Alexis Farrah (George's daughter) for their continued interest and encouragement in writing my book. I also appreciate the frequent telephone calls that my brother Victor has made urging me to continue with my writing when other professional commitments intervened and caused considerable delay in completing this work.

Finally, this book would never have materialized without the expert typing and formatting skills of Ms. Ann E. Anderson, Office Manager of the School of Graduate Studies at SCSU. I extend my thanks and gratitude to her for her continuous, outstanding work and loyalty on my behalf for over twenty-five years.

George A. Farrah

St. Cloud, Minnesota
August 1, 2006

CONTENTS

PROLOGUE

PART I: THE ETHICAL CHOICES

EPILOGUE

LIST OF TABLES

LIST OF FIGURES

INTRODUCTION

"It is better to be divided by truth than to be united by error." – Martin Luther

In many ways, this work does not resemble the usual approach or format for a work of this nature. For example, it is not merely the collection of ideas from other books–as important as that may be. In fact, the title itself may be misleading. When I finally decided on *Images of the West: Portraits in Diversity*, I had in mind a holistic approach of phenomena associated with many disciplines, rather than one particular historical, sociological, or economic view. In effect, then, my thinking has been influenced by a multitude of theoretical frameworks and processes from that vast reservoir of Western ideas.

Of course, there is also the influence of practical events, those first hand experiences that do much to shape one's belief system. In this respect, I remember well those formative collegiate years, both undergraduate and graduate, at Wayne State University. It was there, after my return from overseas military service in World War II that I became keenly interested in the ideas of common core values, especially within a community setting.[1]

Later, both as a university professor and director of graduate level field study research, I received several research grants which allowed me to pursue the aforesaid interests. Since the content areas for much of this inquiry was in the social sciences, the first probe involved determining characteristics of the American Way of Life. In fact, it was at Wayne State University, during the Spring Quarter of 1963, that the original categories and items for a questionnaire were formulated. I remember that, in many ways, the process was slow, and it was like pulling teeth!

For example, I was then on the part-time graduate staff, and, during the course of a day, it took considerable time to obtain the cooperative assistance of numerous scholars in appropriate fields of specialties. Gradually, with the help of a team of graduate students, a body of information took shape.

Basically, the initial step for validation was to determine the types of categories which would adequately describe the American Way of Life. Ultimately, while admittedly quite arbitrary, it was agreed to include the categories of government, economics, science, education, cultural aspects, mass media, and religion. Thus, by the year 1975, the stage was set to survey opinions of various publics at strategic locations throughout the United States.[2]

The subject matter chosen for each chapter results not only from the aforesaid research conducted in our country, but also from selected samples in Europe. Since I was greatly restricted in terms of limited funds, personnel to assist me, and time, my samples involved individuals from universities in Germany and Spain.[3]

Considerable effort had been made by linguists in the areas of German and Spanish to ensure that the translation of the survey items would maximize clarity and understanding.[4] The initial thrust of the U.S. study was to study the relationship of opinions between individuals designated as experts (i.e., those leaders who espouse the morals in the above categories) versus those individuals designated as lay publics (i.e., our citizens who follow the mores in our way of life). In passing, it should be noted that the results of the 1978 research indicated an agreement of 84 percent between the lay publics and experts samples in the U.S.[5]

During a sabbatical leave in 1982, and having received my third university research grant, I went to Europe that year in order to conduct further research in Germany and Spain. In this effort, my research methodology involved interviews with certain leaders in the same areas or categories utilized in the earlier study.[6] With the assistance of the University Research Committee at St. Cloud State University, suggestions were made to help narrow the focus of these interviews. In effect, only one or two questions were selected from each category, and the person interviewed was allowed as much time as he or she needed to answer the question. For example, I asked a question from the category of government which stated: "How do you react to the ideas that 'People should run the government'?"[7]

Others that were interviewed in Germany and Spain included a director of a research institute; a nuclear scientist; the president of an electronics firm; a medical doctor; two school administrators; a high school teacher; and a lawyer. These in-depth interviews afforded me valuable insights of the nature of the responses I had obtained via the questionnaire-survey method, especially in relation to key items such as the one described above.

By 1986, with continuous small sampling throughout our country, twenty-five items emerged that were unanimous in terms of agreement, disagreement, and indecision. This cross-impact analysis of the items versus categories found the most consistency to occur in Education, followed in descending order by Cultural Aspects, Economics, Religion, Mass Media, Government, and Science.

For the most part, these twenty-five items were like catalytic agents that provided me with the ideas for the contents of each chapter. I was then able to integrate these ideas with my readings, travel experiences, and extensive interviewing. Therefore, the chapters were not selected on an arbitrary basis, but follow a more orderly pattern suggested by my research.

In terms of the format for this book, there is a "Prologue" followed by Part I, and an "Epilogue" followed by Part II, and the end notes for each part and the appendixes. Most important, the concept of an "Ethical Choice" is one that seems to permeate all aspects of Western Life.[8] For example, I employ this latter concept because it describes what one <u>does</u> for the best interests of the group rather than simply what one <u>is</u>. It is really the dominant theme in Part I, providing the unifying or integrative aspects of the various topics treated in each chapter.

If past is prologue, then there are numerous generalizations and relationships that have implications for the future of the West. If we are to survive as a resilient, unified nation, the morals, values, mores, practices, and conventions inherent in our American Way of Life will need drastic modifications in this twenty-first century. In fact, I have developed sixteen components of culture, including the latter ones of morals, mores, practices, and conventions. Most sections in each chapter will feature an illustration depicting the components of culture related to the theme of each section. For example, the choice is made between a <u>practice</u> and a <u>sentiment</u> in the area of education. Moreover, as the title suggests—"Portraits in Diversity" involves choices that we make in terms of our values and experiences. Therefore, the concept of diversity takes on a different meaning by giving emphasis to a diversity of interests, a diversity of talent, etc., rather than the current interpretations of diversity. In effect, diversity can become divisive in the categories of the American Way of Life! Reflecting the aforesaid cultural components or topics, each chapter provides the content, sequence, and integration of ideas for this book.

Finally, whether we are able to move away with our obsession with the immediate need for instant gratification and hedonistic practices–especially after the tragic events of September 11– remains to be seen. The Epilogue, includes the Summary and Conclusions followed by three appendices. These two parts, then, under Prologue and Epilogue, respectively, form the crux and the unifying elements of this contribution; hopefully a careful blending of longitudinal research findings–some esoteric and some not–with my experiences.

Next, the subtopics developed in Chapter 1 describe the factors contributing to the Atomization of Culture.

Endnotes for Introduction

[1] My encounters with diverse peoples in Australia, New Guinea, The Dutch East Indies, and the Philippine Islands provided me with new insights regarding common core values. For example, when I was stationed briefly in Sidney, Australia, I discovered that the Australians share many of the values inherent in our American Way of Life.

[2] Via a university-sponsored research grant from St. Cloud State University (SCSU) which was awarded to me, and with the assistance of several institutions of higher learning across America and professors at my own university, I surveyed over 1300 students at eighteen universities or colleges regarding these specified categories (i.e., government, economics, education, etc.). The findings resulting from this research effort were included in my publication entitled: A Study of the American Way of Life, Volumes I to III, St. Cloud State University Printing Services, 478 pp., St. Cloud, MN, June 17, 1977.

[3] Another funded research project from SCSU allowed me the funds and time to conduct this research in Europe.

[4] Ibid.

[5] See Volume II of the American Way of Life.

[6] During 1982, I took my third trip to Europe in order to replicate my initial effort.

[7] From these data, I was later able to make a comparative analysis between my American samples and those from Germany and Switzerland. While in Germany and Switzerland, in addition to some key items, I conducted interviews with leaders concerning their transportation system—particularly their excellent passenger railroad systems. Their results or opinions are included in the final section of Chapter One dealing with "Transportation: Its Availability and Reliability" (i.e., in America).

[8] These ethical choices involve our everyday life and in those seven categories of the American Way of Life.

CHAPTER ONE

THE ATOMIZATION OF CULTURE

The sub-topics that are described in this chapter are dynamically related to the central theme of a macro perspective of American culture–a residual of the Western form, with its historical European/Greco-Roman origin. Even though there may be considerable overlap in the themes, each sub-topic contains concepts, generalizations, and relationships which are designed to aid the reader in better understanding the complex issues inherent in this macro view of culture. For example, later in this chapter, the key concepts involved in the components of a culture are demonstrated via a three-dimensional chart. Since all of these sub-topics are vital to a better understanding of culture, it is difficult to prioritize them in their order of importance. Therefore, since the concept of culture is a dominant theme for the ideas expressed in my book, it is considered first.

Some Components of Culture

This misapplication of the word "culture" is evident by the definition provided by a new generation of social scientists or others. Therefore, this interpretation, reinforced by authors of college undergraduate and graduate textbooks dealing with societal organization, has become the new fashionable description to use.[1] Consequently, "culture" has been fragmented and atomized into a utilitarian use of the moment for the sake of convenience.

This dramatic change in meaning is apparent when it is quite common to hear or see in print many examples of this distorted or misused concept. For example, leaders of organizations, newspaper columnists, educators at every level, business personnel, and a host of others have contributed to this distortion. One is amazed at the glib readiness of these (who should know better) individuals when they use "culture" to describe, in reality, <u>a practice, sentiment, or convention</u>, or as illustrated_and defined later, other components of culture! Thus, from the business world, to educational institutions of higher learning, and to a variety of other groups or persons, we have seen this concept applied.

In my own case, some years ago, when I was teaching a graduate course concerning the dynamics of organization, the text we were using contained this statement, "Both the cards and the awards help make Ford's culture thicker by exposing employees and dealers to a core value, customer satisfaction."[2] Then, recently, a university professor discussed the "culture of hanging" in a letter to the editor of our local newspaper; and in another edition of the same newspaper, this phrase was used as a heading to the article: "Colleges' 'culture of drinking' kills 1400 each year."

Unfortunately, these misapplications of "culture" are intimately associated with a cultural relevance which is heavily laden with distortions and contradictions. For example, on the one hand, a respected scholar writes, "The study of man's many and varied cultures indicate that in this regard all human beings are alike. Further, while there are differences among class, religious, national and racial groups, all are part of a total

'American culture.'" While this macro view is satisfactory, on the other hand, the same author, in the same article, makes this contradictory statement: "One can speak of this 'culture' of different institutions—hospitals have different 'cultures' on the whole from schools and both from business houses." Continuing with this <u>micro</u> view of culture it is stated that there is even a 'classroom culture.'

Therefore, in the latter examples I believe that the word <u>practice</u>, instead of "culture," would be more accurate or appropriate. As an illustration of the various dimensions of culture as a <u>macro concept</u> involving several layers both horizontally and vertically, the components of a culture can be visualized within a three dimensional model as shown in Figure 1. For example, how do individuals or members of a group belonging to our culture give articulation or expression to their life experiences? From this model below, one can best understand these dynamic entities in terms of their level of social organization; trait patterns; control patterns; and verbal applications. These latter entities—referred to as A, B, C, and D—interact both vertically and horizontally.

First, let us consider the "Levels of Social Organization." From Figure 1 it can be noted that all of the letter A's form a vertical arrangement which include these components: 1) Societal; 2) Group; 3) Personal; and 4) Self. From this particular, vertical column on the far left, these levels indicate <u>less</u> social compulsion to conform. Yet, by moving upward in columns A, B, C, and D, each level becomes more generalized and vague!

Second, column A, already defined in the above paragraph, included the components for the "Level of Social Organization." In a similar manner, the components for the B column are the "Trait Patterns" of a culture and include: 1) Conventions; 2) Folkways; 3) Traits; and 4) Attitudes.[3]

9

Components of a Culture

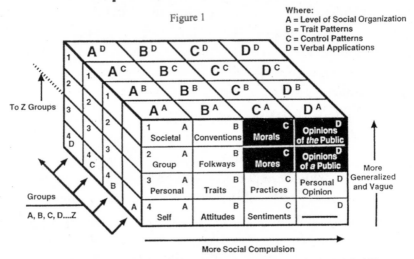

Figure 1

Where:
A = Level of Social Organization
B = Trait Patterns
C = Control Patterns
D = Verbal Applications

Adapted from The Shaping and Reshaping Forces of Acculturation: A Study of Risk, George Farrah © 1993, St. Coud, MN.

Third, and it is a most significant column which leads to more social compulsion, column C contains the components of "Control Patterns." These include our 1) Morals; 2) Mores; 3) Practices; and 4) Sentiments. A more detailed explanation of this column as well as the others is provided below.[4]

Fourth, these components of a culture are reflected within groups A, B, C, D, to Z groups in our American Way of Life, from profit and non-profit organizations, to states, and to communities or cities. It may be noted that the conventions, folkways, traits, attitudes, morals, mores, practices, and sentiments provide—as it were—the social cement that holds or binds these groups together. The stronger the bond, the greater the cultural vitality. Conversely, the weaker the bond, there is a lessening of cultural vitality. Therefore, the growing emphasis on aspects or issues of diversity, in turn, promotes a greater <u>heterogeneity</u>. **Since our common core values are the ingredients from which the social cement is formed, the relative strength of cultural vitality is affected.**

Finally, since a dominant characteristic of our culture features democratic practices, the groups or individuals who make up the American Way of Life are allowed the freedom to articulate their opinions. Thus, for the components in column D, "Verbal Applications" are typical for three levels and include: 1) Opinions of the Public; 2) Opinions of a Public; 3) Personal Opinion; and 4) a blank entry which is explained below.

A more intensive analysis of these cultural components reveals these generalizations:

1. That on level one—the most generalized and vague—people appear as they should be. (Here, they wear a kind of "cultural cloak.")

2. That on level two, where trait patterns occur, people appear as they have to be.

3. That on level three, the control patterns, people appear as they seem to be, and

4. On level four, where more covert characteristics are evident in three columns out of four, people appear as they really are.

5. Finally, it should be observed that the blackened areas in Columns C and D for levels 1 and 2 (i.e., Morals, Mores, and Opinions of the Public , Opinions of a Public respectively) are given special emphases. In the first instance, there is a great distance now in our way of life between "what should be" (i.e., morals) and "what is" (i.e., mores). Secondly, the shaping forces of mass media and television also reveal a growing distance between these two forms of opinions—the public and a public.

Moreover, in terms of the fourth level, which is the least generalized and vague, one may be curious as to why the "self" at column D is left blank. It is left blank because one can never be certain of a person's deeply seated attitude or social value; and because, on this particular level, there is more social compulsion to conform. For example, if someone asked me about a certain issue which inwardly I did not agree, in order to gain social approval, I could circumvent the issue by expressing an opinion of agreement. However, that opinion does not really reflect my deepest seated attitude![5]

Within this same vein, it would be erroneous to conclude that, merely because one has surveyed or sampled a given group, attitudes are necessarily obtained. Collectively, it may be said that on the group level, there are many publics in our heterogeneous societies. Their expression of opinions reflect their particular group, folkways, and mores on this second horizontal level.

Note also the blackened areas of column C. Herein, a gulf exists between our morals (i.e., the "should be") and our mores (i.e., our folkways of feeling, thinking, and acting conducive to the welfare or survival of our society). This distinction between morals and mores is crucial in understanding the concept of the loss of cultural vitality. The greater the gap between these two dynamic entities reveals the distance between what "should be" versus "what actually exists." Since our leaders shape these morals in terms of their purity of purpose and truthfulness, their ethical choices are guided by the extent that their behavior reflects this purity of purpose and truthfulness. **Therefore, the greater the gap, the greater the loss of cultural vitality.** The blackened area in Figure 1 is repeated for each section that follows in all chapters because of the gap in the cultural components in columns C and D.

Finally, this form of cultural relativism has been applied to the business world; to educational institutions of higher learning or school districts; and to a variety of other groups. One example from the world of business will suffice: "Both the cards and the awards help make Ford's culture thicker by exposing

12

employees and dealers to a core value, customer satisfaction."[6] It is noteworthy to compare this latter utilitarian definition of culture with that given by an American Indian from Red Lake, Minnesota. He gave this definition of culture:

The dynamics of a group of people makes them be who they are. It includes the historical, the transition period, and the contemporary. Culture, in this respect reflects the values of a people and is expressed through their religion, music, art, literature, and technology.[7]

In summary, the components of culture described in this section provide a more complete picture of societal organizational indices in a macro sense rather than a narrow approach. The implications for our educational process are enormous and give meaning to the vital role of acculturation. An elaboration of this vital role is examined in the next section.

Education as Crises Management:
Fruits of the Industrial Concept of Education

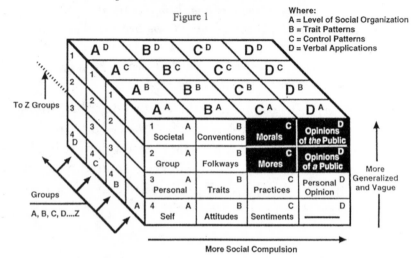

Components of a Culture

Figure 1

Where:
A = Level of Social Organization
B = Trait Patterns
C = Control Patterns
D = Verbal Applications

Adapted from The Shaping and Reshaping Forces of Acculturation: A Study of Risk, George Farrah © 1993, St. Coud, MN.

1A Societal	3A Personal
2A Group	4A Self

Early in the twentieth century youth would learn that culture was defined as the sum total of society's experience, both material and non-material. Of special significance to education was the contribution that R. Freeman Butts made in terms of a cultural history. The anthropological meaning he provided (circa 1947) was not restricted to a literary or artistic sense, as important as these humanistic areas are. Rather, he defined it as the institutions that a society lived by: political, economic, social, and religious.[8] In addition to these four categories, over a period of time, I added three more: science, education, and mass media. Thus, these seven categories became

the basis for my research relating to the American Way of Life—
"a residual society of the Western Culture."

Quite clearly, in the shaping-reshaping process of education,
the content areas inherent in units of teaching are broad in scope
to address both general and specific objectives. Therefore, the
content areas of literature, social sciences, and science encompass
a tremendous amount of cultural information! Interestingly
enough, the earlier definition of culture provided by Chuck
Robinson is not unique because it echoes a similar macro
interpretation given at the early stages of the twentieth century.
It was the eminent educational philosopher, John Dewey, who
described how a culture–really the process of acculturation–
interacts in a "mode of association" with the school.[9] In his view,
education involved three functions. First, since the acculturation
process is "too complex to be assimilated in total," it has to be
broken up into portions, as it were, and "assimilated piecemeal
in a gradual and graded way."

Therefore, this first function of education is vital because it
involves passing on our values and heritage via the process of
acculturation.

As a second function, he asserted that "it is the business of the
school environment to eliminate, as far as possible, the unworthy
features of the existing environment from influenced upon
mental habitudes." Thus, in making for a better society of the
future, the school is the main social agency for accomplishing
this goal.

Finally, for his third function of the school, Dewey believed
that it was the mission of the school to "balance the various
elements in the social environment . . . to see to it that each
individual gets an opportunity to escape from the limitations of
the social group in which he was born." In retrospect, and in
view of this latter function, his belief in the school's mission was

validated in the late 1950's and early 1960's. It was during these years that the federal government and many states innovated the practice of <u>compensatory education</u> in order to assist those children who were disadvantaged or "culturally deprived." For example, in many urban centers free breakfasts and free lunches for the disadvantaged children from low income families became a common practice and it continues today.

The latter generalizations are crucial for the educator in understanding the acculturation process. Historically as discovery, invention, and growth have gradually increased the complexity of our cultural organization, so education has increased in size, scope, and organization. For example, the emergence of the national state in the nineteenth century, particularly in its pluralistic development, brought education into greater prominence, and has resulted in the development to a large degree of federal and state control and more specific organization.

It was necessary because education has always been associated with a political structure and organization upon which local boards of education depend. Unfortunately, because, more often than not, the appropriating legislative body or governor, confronted with social or financial pressures–intimately related to the polemics of the political world according to its ranking of priorities–reduces the funds allocated to school districts. Those districts involved have no choice but to reduce their funding for programs, staff, building programs, or materials.

Therein is the grave risk: the state has become the source of considerable funding for the operation of local units. If <u>the budget allows for it</u>, states can be very generous in their commitments and their allocations. However, with state funding now being tied in with the ability of professional teaching staffs and their schools to meet the standards set by the state, many of our schools–especially those in large urban centers with large numbers of minority students from kindergarten to senior high school–are presently experiencing the negative impact of reduced funding. Then to further confound the issue of funding for public schools, the voucher movement, where parents can elect to send their children to charter schools, threatens the very existence of free, public education.

Apparently, parents take these alternative measures because they are dissatisfied with teaching methods or the school's curricula—especially the cognitive skills in the content areas of literature (i.e., reading and the other language arts), science, and the social sciences or social studies. Parents are dissatisfied because their educational sentiments are at variances with the practices of educators. In Table 1, one can note this contrast in expectations between the community and the school.

In the next section, a constellation of ideas relating to propaganda, reactions to it, and two kinds of opinions are considered.

Table 1

Comparison of Various Issues Between the Community and Education*

	THE COMMUNITY	EDUCATORS
	1. Cognitive.	1. Cognitive, affective, psychomotor.
	2. Eight hours of work equals eight hours.	2. Five hours of school work may equal eight hours of physical work.
	3. Modified form of the family.	3. The family as supportive, as a source for information or communication about the child.
Some important issues or expectations such as: sources of support, interest; involvement; or other pertinent comparisons.	4. Increasing skepticism about the support of public schooling.	4. Continued dependence on the local board and the state for financial support.
	5. Active or hidden antagonism toward the school.	5. Conditional antagonism regarding the lack of understanding of the educational mission.
	6. Increased demands on the teachers' time and effort.	6. With cutbacks in staff, more and more assumed roles.
	7. Immediate success; everyone should be educated, "no child left behind."	7. In the latent development of maturation every child cannot be educated the same way. (The extent of future success or failure for most children or youth is uncertain.)
	8. Emphasis on the "What."	8. Emphasis on the "How."
	9. Product oriented.	9. Persons, products, processes, and properties of the mind oriented.

Articulate Propaganda versus Sensory Reactions:
Knowledge by Intuition

Components of a Culture

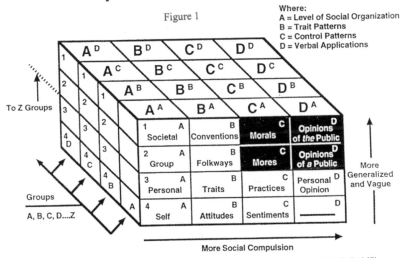

Figure 1

Where:
A = Level of Social Organization
B = Trait Patterns
C = Control Patterns
D = Verbal Applications

Adapted from The Shaping and Reshaping Forces of Acculturation: A Study of Risk, George Farrah © 1993, St. Coud, MN.

3B Traits	1D Opinions of *the* Public
4B Attitudes	2D Opinions of *a* Public

As it will be observed from the above cultural components extracted from column D of Figure 1, shown above, the opinions expressed by <u>the Public</u> tend to be more generalized and vague than those given by <u>a Public</u>. Nevertheless, in both instances, the formal, structured sources that shape these opinions emanate from articulate propaganda of the mass media. These media sources range from television to radio, to newspapers, to publications, and to a host of less formal sources. For example, in the most recent war with Iraq, millions of Americans representing <u>the Public</u> (i.e., the extensive number of groups in our country and elsewhere in the world) responded to the shaping forces of opinions from the mass media in order to support our leadership and troops. In contrast, while in the minority, thousands of dissidents who belonged to groups constituting <u>a Public</u>, were not in agreement with those shaping forces and were opposed to this war for a multitude of reasons. In this latter case, articulate propaganda, with its claims to objective reporting or coverage of information in terms of practices, ideas, doctrines, or sentiments, was highly successful. Yet, for thousands of intelligent and perceptive American citizens, the facts or coverage of information articulated by our political leadership and given wide coverage by the mass media, were open to question. Equally important, these shaping forces of propaganda were not congruent with their deeply seated traits and attitudes. Fortunately, in our country, where democracy flourishes, citizens can question the acts or decisions made by their leaders, at any level of government, without fear of reprisals. Accordingly, in the recent military strike against Iraq, two dominant reasons or themes were given for our justification: 1) that "weapons of mass destruction" were there; and 2) that somehow the Iraqi leadership had connections with the horrible September 11th attack on the World Trade Center buildings in New York City as well as the Pentagon by terrorists. Consider that these two themes, repeated constantly, over and over again by the media until they bore the stamp of credibility, could well be a gross distortion of the true facts—if and when they become known. Consider also that, for the first time in our history, we have conducted a pre-emptive military action on really (at best) circumstantial evidence!

Therefore, it is tragic to witness the absence of <u>bona fide</u> dissent; and that true dialogue regarding the crucial issues has been ignored in favor of simplistic discussion. Persons who disagree on issues of war versus peaceful alternatives should be encouraged to disagree rather than the self-righteousness inherent in a narrow view or opinion. Most important, in no way does this honest dissent diminish or take away the need to give our total support to those brave men and women who are risking their lives for our country![10]

Perhaps, in the reshaping process of opinions found in the opinions of a Public (i.e., a particular group united in their dissent of the articulated propaganda), knowledge by intuition can be a key factor. Here, I am not referring to what is often labeled as "a woman's intuition," but rather to the immediately apprehended feeling that something is amiss, that something has been distorted, simply because the articulated message defies one's common sense and evaluation of the "facts" involved.[11] Unlike our western culture, where the practice of logic, reason, and rational thought has been dominant, many groups or individuals from eastern cultures arrive at knowledge in a different manner. Equally important is the realization that any distortion that is apparent from the articulated propaganda could violate our practices, sentiments, conventions, or traditions.

In terms of mass communications, it is interesting to note that the Internet has shifted the balance of power in relation to who controls the information we receive. Unfortunately, in the past, those who controlled the medias did so in order to emphasize their own opinions or viewpoints. On the other hand, the advent of the Internet made it less expensive for the entrepreneur to get into the business. Consequently, there was a higher level of competition among the sources of media. As a profound development for the process of interaction, the Internet has become a valuable technique for reshaping any distortion of information coming boldly from the shaping forces of the mass media.

Since the Internet represents a tremendous advance in communications technology in its speed and pervasiveness, it is important to know that quality of the message. For example, in the hierarchy of communications, there are four levels, and, from the lowest level to the highest, these are data, information, knowledge, and wisdom. Therefore, what is commonly known as the "explosion of knowledge," is, in reality, the explosion of all kinds of grouped or ungrouped data or information. Of course, data and information are vital in our highly sophisticated computer age and they are indispensable in the conduct of business everywhere especially the global network of communications. However, even though a civilization progresses when it is simpler or easier to convey a message, the aforesaid distinction between the two lower levels (i.e., data and information) versus the two higher levels (i.e., knowledge and wisdom) is essential to understanding the computer's role in our daily lives—especially its role in education.

Historically, consider the impact that Johannes Gutenberg had during the mid-1400's. During those days, before he developed the printing press, scholars and monks in the Catholic Church dedicated years of service copying texts by hand and decorating them with illuminated pages.[12] Now, with Gutenberg's dynamic innovation, written works or books could be reproduced in great numbers—with both speed and accuracy. Now it was possible for the common man (and perhaps, some women) to gain access to <u>bona fide</u> knowledge, whether to read a copy of a bible in his/her own language or some other printed book of interest.

In contrast or comparison to Gutenberg's great impact and influence on Western culture—particularly on the Reformation which followed—the technological advances of the twentieth century laid the scientific foundations for the present electronic revolution of the computer and the Internet systems. However, similar to learning to read when it was not fashionable or possible for so many to do so, the computer requires certain skills in order to cope and apply those skills via the Internet. Most important in this most efficient form of communication, **for the most part it is really data and information that is communicated!**

As it was noted above, since data and information belong to the lower levels of the communication process, they may be characterized as the immediate form. In contrast, knowledge and wisdom, belonging to the higher levels, are of the latent form. Therefore, being latent, they require more time and reflection in a qualitative setting rather than the quantitative speed of a computer message such as the email or eletter. This synthetic thought is quicker than the human mind in its electronic ability to transmit information. Quite clearly, in the dawn of this twenty-first century, we have literally unimaginable power locked up in the small space that the computer requires for its enormous power and potential.

With the aforesaid possibilities and limitations in mind, the dramatic entry of computers into classrooms or labs at all levels—from early elementary grades to institutions of higher learning—are being incorporated into the curriculum content areas of science, literature and the social sciences.

In terms of the above content areas—really the backbone of the curriculum and the passing on of our multicultural heritage—coping, interacting and applying knowledge is most essential for learning. Excellent computer programs have been created and are available for teaching units in the content areas; however, interaction by the student with the teacher and others must occur. It is in this manner that the teacher-learning process becomes personal, dynamic, and active. The idea of a "virtual reality" made possible via electronic communication is a form of synthetic thought as is "artificial intelligence," at once quicker than our own thoughts. Imagine: with this highly sophisticated technique, the child or adult is able to reshape the intended communication so that understanding can lead to the latent form—knowledge and wisdom.

Consider another concrete example illustrating the sharp contrast between immediate and latent communications. For example, in a validated nationwide study which also involved European samples, these steps were employed in the comparative analysis. First, data were collected and analyzed, via the computer, and, as a result, produced valuable information regarding the sub-groups being evaluated. Second, the transformation process from information to knowledge required a <u>dialogue</u> to occur between this author and several experts in related fields.[13] As a result of this dialogue, knowledge was shared and wisdom enhanced within those involved.

It should also be noted that a cyclical effort is occurring in this latter transformation process because knowledge and wisdom can be fed back and shared with the community at large. Thus, this important distinction or contrast between immediate and latent forms provides a new approach to the interaction process.

In summary, this section considered the dichotomy between opinions of <u>the public</u> versus opinions of <u>a public</u> of opinions ranging from television to radio, and to many less formal sources. If these above sources are regarded as the shaping forces of opinions directed to the public at large, then the reshaping forces reflect opinions expressed by a group or personal opinion. Very often, there is disagreement–sometimes intense–between the shaping and reshaping forces. However, these differences are normal and are to be expected in our American Way of Life.

While the Internet has caused a powerful impact on the speed and pervasiveness in communications, its value concerns data and information in an immediate modality. When the more latent form of knowledge and wisdom are considered, a structure of communication resulted: the former are the lower levels and the latter the higher levels. Within general education and the specific classroom, an increasing reliance or dependence has been given to computer technology as an aid in instruction. Yet, without the process of interacting, the skills of coping and applying are affected in negative ways.[14]

In the next section, attention is directed to the drastic changes that have occurred in the family, especially the changing roles and its impact on the atomization of culture.

The Myth of the Family: Changing Roles

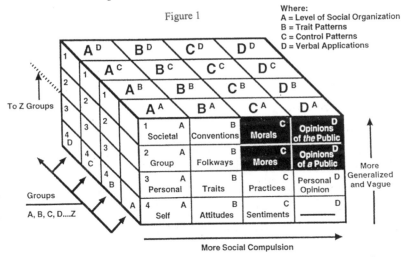

Components of a Culture

Figure 1

Where:
A = Level of Social Organization
B = Trait Patterns
C = Control Patterns
D = Verbal Applications

To Z Groups

Groups

A, B, C, D....Z

	1 A Societal	B Conventions	C Morals	D Opinions of *the* Public
	2 A Group	B Folkways	C Mores	D Opinions of *a* Public
	3 A Personal	B Traits	C Practices	Personal D Opinion
	4 A Self	B Attitudes	C Sentiments	D

More
Generalized
and Vague

More Social Compulsion

Adapted from The Shaping and Reshaping Forces of Acculturation: A Study of Risk, George Farrah © 1993, St. Coud, MN.

1B Conventions	3C Practices
2B Folkways	4C Sentiments

Without question, of all traditions within the American Way of Life, the structure of the family has experienced profound changes. Therefore, in describing these changes, this section will examine the conventions and folkways as well as practices and sentiments concerning the changing roles of the family.

As a point of entry or reference to the "Components of a Culture" shown above in Figure 1, the reader can relate Conventions and Folkways to Column B where these components are more generalized in agreements between persons on the usages or habits of their social life. Conversely, Practices and Sentiments in Column C have more specificity, and where these components tend to be more compulsion in social arrangements.[15]

Accordingly, the first attribute concerns the concepts which designate these changing roles. For example, the concepts of father, mother, husband, wife, have given way to different meanings or interpretations. Since the divorce rate has accelerated during the last few decades, one finds single mothers or single fathers at the head of a family rather than a husband and his wife. Now, in contrast, it is common practice for many couples to share the same living quarters with a "live in boyfriend" or a "live in girlfriend," often having children within this arrangement. The sentiment of commitment, which is the foundation of a bona fide marriage embellished and strengthened by vows, may or may not be present in such an arrangement. If not, then what can prevent one or the other from leaving in favor of another alternative or arrangement? When children are part of this setting, what are the psychological and social effects that impact them?

The prevalence of these changing roles are so extensive in our family structure that volumes of books, guides and other materials have been written about these changes. From professionals such as psychiatrists, sociologists, school counselors, religious leaders, to political leaders or media commentaries and columnists, a wealth of information has been generated. Yet, despite the knowledge and wisdom inherent in the morals, traditions and values of our multicultural heritage, certain ethical choices have been ignored or replaced with a neutral relativism.

In their analysis of the practice of marriage, for example, sociologists and other scholars observe that remaining unmarried is no longer considered disgraceful–even when a couple share the same living quarters. Apparently the social pressure still remains, but the imperative to marry is weaker today than ever before in our history. Therefore, with the prevailing mores, even if people desire to marry, they do not feel any sentiment to do so. Yet, the basis for endearing or long lasting relationships–marriage or otherwise–is the sentiment of love. The ethical choice of commitment is not always related to love, however desirable to any given couple. Thus, when commitment is absent but love is declared, a relationship becomes conditional–one can leave the other at a moment's notice!

What, then, is the quality of this love which provides the bond of cement between two persons? Is it the agape kind which is spiritual and suprapersonal–beyond the mere self? Assuredly, depending on the person, place, time or historical setting, its meaning and interpretation will vary. However, in terms of the family, this sentiment of love is crucial for its healthy survival.

In their perceptive analysis of love and the self, Robert Bellah–the eminent sociologist–and his associates have studied this relationship. For example, over thirty years ago, they discovered that a "1970 survey found that 91 percent of all Americans held to the ideal of two people sharing a life and a home together". When the same question was asked in 1980, the same percentage agreed. Yet when a national sample was asked in 1978 whether 'most couples getting married today expect to remain married for the rest of their lives,' 60 percent said no. Love and commitment, it appears are desirable, but not easy."[16] Bellah also contends (and I agree) that "in addition to believing in love, we Americans believe in the self" which often causes conflict in the normal interactions or points of tension encountered in the best of marriages.[17]

More recently, the practice of marriage, has been severely tested by the shaping factors of economics and social conditions. It has been reported that, by the year 2002, the number of unmarried couples living together was 5.5 million, an increase of 4,977,000 couples or 90.0 percent more than was reported in 1970–just over thirty years ago.[18]

Moreover, in my research of The American Way of Life which was conducted from April 1975 to October 1987 (i.e., see Appendix A for more detailed information about comparable items used in samples from the United States, Germany, and Spain), there were eight items related to the category of "Cultural Aspects," one of seven categories. Herein, one finds the various aspects which indirectly reflect the changing roles in marriage. For example, using a five point Likert response system ranging from "Strongly Disagree" to "Strongly Agree," with "Undecided" as the middle three values, the respondents totaling 1578– representing all ages, regional locations, and gender-related the following four items in this unanimous manner with a brief interpretation for each item:

Item (N = 1578)   Response

4.0   Women should marry by age 20.   <u>Disagree</u>

- Quite clearly, this practice was a normal occurrence in the nineteenth century, but, with the advent of the Women's Suffrage Movement, the Women's Liberation and Feminist Movements, this sentiment or response changed with the approach of the twentieth century. The movement from rural to urban settings may have also been a factor.

6.0   A woman's place is in the home.   <u>Disagree</u>

- In contrast to the males role as the provider and head of the household, the female role centered on the domestic duties of cooking, laundering clothes, and other tasks in the home including the care of children. Then, with the advent of voting rights, educational opportunities, and leadership roles in politics, the business world, and other fields, the gains for women have been tremendous! However, most women in leadership roles lag behind men in terms of pay for their services.

61   A family that plays together stays
      together.   <u>Undecided</u> (90%)
                                       <u>Agree</u> (10%)

- As a bonding agent for the survival of the family, being together for various kinds of enjoyable activities involves a high level of interaction. With the demands of work for the parents and schooling for the children, the factors of time, space, and flexibility are of prime importance. In view of the latter pressures, it is not surprising that the influence and power of television, personal computers, electronic game playing, or other individual activities affect the process of interaction. As noted above from my survey of this particular practice, only 10% of those samples agreed with this item. Without doubt, the majority were unsure of how to respond to this statement.

68. Children reflect the home environment. Agree (100%)

- The shaping forces of the home via the type of modeling provided by the parents or guardians are most significant in the development of personality and character in children. If there is confusion over what family life should be like in the home, role expectations can be in a constant state of flux. For example, the beginnings of a mature personality are nurtured by the interrelationships of such aspects as security and safety in terms of nutritional needs, emotional stability, and the ability to cope, interact, and apply many kinds of skills.[19]

In summary, the dominant characteristics described in this section regarding the changing roles in the family are intimately related to the quality of marriage, the activities chosen by the family, and the modeling provided by the parents or guardians.

Within the categories specified earlier for The American Way of Life (i.e., government, cultural aspects, education, etc.), critical issues have become apparent. The issue of justice versus power is considered in the next section.

Issues of Polarity: Justice versus Power

Components of a Culture

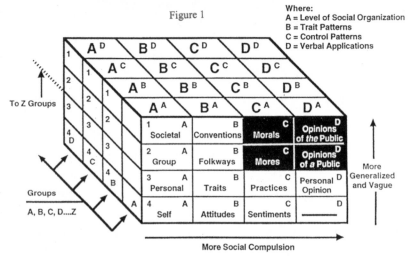

Figure 1

Where:
A = Level of Social Organization
B = Trait Patterns
C = Control Patterns
D = Verbal Applications

Adapted from The Shaping and Reshaping Forces of Acculturation: A Study of Risk, George Farrah © 1993, St. Coud, MN.

1C Morals
2C Mores

Although the more generalized component of morals involves the ethical choices of right and wrong, it also conveys the latent meaning of "what should be," these are items or concerns that are often not clear or concise. Conversely, the less generalized component of mores implies the immediate "what is," and these mores are really those folkways of feeling, thinking, and acting that are necessary for the survival of the group.[20]

Quite clearly, in our American way of life, there is a dichotomy or distance between the "should be" and the "is," or the immediately apprehended. Increasingly, it seems, especially in the matter of income, there is a growing distance between our once dominant middle class and those Americans who are more affluent. In fact, a once thriving middle class is now hard to identify—if it exists at all! Yet, it is a paradox that if asked what social class a typical American belongs to, that person, regardless of wealth or social status, will reply: "I belong to the middle class." How ironic that is!

As indicated in the previous section, the family, already weakened by several shaping forces, has been further weakened by the polarity described above. For millions of Americans who struggle daily to eke out a living, they have grave concerns for their own welfare as well as the future of our country. They are concerned because they see the loss of thousands of jobs which are now in foreign countries. As a result, with the current emphasis of our government on a global economy, great numbers of American employees at all levels in our country are simply no longer employed.[21] Nevertheless, in all fairness to our corporations, where the margin of profits continue to diminish, they have sought and discovered marketplaces in the world where their products can be manufactured cheaper. Our corporations also struggle to survive!

Other vital issues cast a shadow of gloom for our citizens concerning their future welfare. To gauge the frequency and range of these issues, all one has to do is to read the public letter box of one's local newspaper. In these opinions expressed publicly, one dominant issue concerns the affordability of health care. As premiums for health insurance plans increase, health care is becoming beyond the reach of an alarming number of our citizens. The frequent increase in premiums cause employers—especially smaller businesses—to cut or eliminate health benefits to their employees. Most tragic, in our great country, thousands of Americans—including the homeless or disenfranchised—are without any insurance whatsoever.

While it is difficult to prioritize the full range of publicly expressed concerns, one notes those concerning education, the national debt, our continued presence in Iraq and its cost in American lives and dollars, affordable housing, and a host of other issues. In terms of coping with those issues that apply to them, both local and state governments across our nation struggle valiantly to find solutions. However, with the endemic budget cuts and downsizing of staff and programs, it becomes most difficult to deal with these issues.

On the national level, where the issues described above are polarized between the two major political parties, legislative progress is slow and tedious. While there are representatives and senators from both parties who should be commended for their sincere and dedicated efforts, the fact remains that far too many legislators are committed to agendas that fail to reflect the needs of their constituents. Since the quality of representation is a key process in our form of democratic government, the process must work in order to resolve issues of concern for our citizens. Otherwise, the representation is severely flawed in this division of power.[22] Therefore, how can justice prevail in a flawed system? Fortunately, it prevails because of the willingness of adversarial parties to compromise on polarized issues.

Strategic planning in our organizations, both profit and non-profit, raises serious questions and this process is examined in the next section.

Immediacy versus Latency: The Myth of Strategic Planning

Components of a Culture

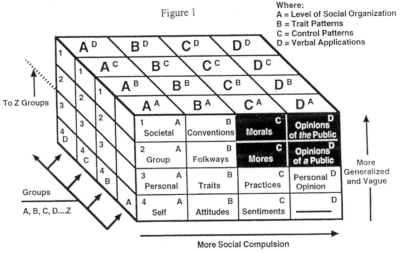

Figure 1

Where:
A = Level of Social Organization
B = Trait Patterns
C = Control Patterns
D = Verbal Applications

	A	B	C	D
1	Societal	Conventions	Morals	Opinions of *the* Public
2	Group	Folkways	Mores	Opinions of *a* Public
3	Personal	Traits	Practices	Personal Opinion
4	Self	Attitudes	Sentiments	—

To Z Groups

Groups A, B, C, D....Z

More Generalized and Vague

More Social Compulsion

Adapted from *The Shaping and Reshaping Forces of Acculturation: A Study of Risk*, George Farrah © 1993, St. Coud, MN.

1A Societal	3C Practices
2A Group	4C Sentiments

One may note that, in planning for the latent future, the shaping and reshaping forces occurred in this manner: new approaches seriously questioned time-honored traditions, institutions, and dogmas. Moreover, in particular, this reshaping of values involved new perceptions about the vastness of the universe; subatomic physics; the insignificance of life; quantum theory; non-Euclidean geometry; relativity; nuclear energy; the "Alpha Helix" of Linus Pauling; and the "Double Helix" of Watson and Crick, which greatly contributed to the science of molecular biology and the discovery of DNA.

If the present is a point of tension between past events and the future, one has to understand the dominant themes or events of the past twentieth century. Consider, for example, the tremendous shaping forces and upheavals in matters political, economic, cultural, and intellectual. The immediate concerns, then, were the problems associated with shifting from a rural, agricultural society to an expanding industrial society. The pains resulting from this process of change were evident in the cyclical economic booms and depressions of unparalleled magnitudes. There were also devastating wars, revolutions, and alarming incidences of nationalistic and racial intolerance. There was also extensive experimentation in art, music, and literature.[23]

Considering the immediate problems in the dawn of this new century which, in particular, confront our country, and, in general the world, it is well to remember the wisdom of Arnold Toynbee, the noted historiographer.[24] This eminent historian had studied and analyzed a total of 26 civilizations from earliest times to the date that he completed his comprehensive analysis. In this succinct analysis, he concluded that 19 of the 26 civilizations were "dead and buried." For his analysis, Toynbee had borrowed two important concepts from modern behavioral psychology: stimulus and response. In addition, he used the thesis of "challenge" and the antithesis of "response" to describe a particular civilization.

Therefore, from Toynbee's vantage ground, it is quite clear that a civilization survives when it is able to respond to the challenges confronting it. In this case, he uses the Eskimos as an example of a surviving civilization, because of their ability to cope with the dangers of a harsh environment and limited resources. The immediate daily struggles of the Eskimo to survive are so intense that little time remains for the more latent leisure activities, such as music, art, or other areas of the humanities. Instead, survival at all costs is the key issue. Is this factor of survival, albeit for different reasons, also an issue today?

Indeed, in present day America, strategic or long-range planning involves many issues concerning our survival. For example, there is the issue of changes in the environment involved in global warming; in atomic waste from the many uses of nuclear energy; the role of our military; planning in business or non-profit organizations; and various levels of government, from local to national. Confronted with these issues, organizational leaders rely on a number of techniques to maximize efficiency and output. For example, one such technique involves goal setting by both employees or departments. However, rather than strategic planning for the latent future, the goal setting process is done on an immediate basis in response to the competitive challenges of the day, week, or month. Thus, goal setting becomes short-ranged, as though it were a hand-to-mouth endeavor! Then to have credibility or success for the goals to be achieved, there must be a commitment to provide the resources, time, and energy in order to realize their attainment. Otherwise, morale in the work place tends to break down when there is an absence of truthfulness and purity of purpose.

Most important, strategic planning requires the attributes of time and flexibility in order to be meaningful. In this connection, I remember how the Danish local government in Fredericia used the process of simulation in the strategic planning of their budget. It involved many groups in the community—especially the various businesses and schools in the region.

Accordingly, for their process of simulating a future budget, the city planner took these steps:

1. In order to determine what items would be included in the City of Fredericia budget, all agencies and departments connected with the operation of the government or social agencies such as the schools were contacted.

2. Via a formal communication, they were requested to itemize their material needs or services for the year ahead—in this instance, 1974-75.

3. The list of needs or services and their estimated cost were then forwarded to the city planner.

4. Having received these requests in the specified time from those involved, the city planner compiled the returned material so that he could present his findings to the City Council members for their collective evaluation.

5. At this stage, the planner and council determined a "goodness of fit" between the designated, proposed budget and the material needs or services indicated by the branches of city government.

6. Therefore, a comparison was made between the estimated available funds and requests that were made.

7. When these data were analyzed, some of the requests were scaled back and the particular agencies involved were notified in sufficient time <u>months before the final budget was approved and became a reality</u>.

This model of simulation greatly diminishes the possibility of disappointment, conflict, or confusion that occurs with emphases on more immediate planning or solutions. For example, imagine the employee or leader, sincere in the stating of needs or goals, discovering that her/his requests could not be met because the financial means were not forthcoming!

Of course, there are other excellent models of strategic planning, but those that feature latent development are superior to those immediate designs; and, they are more likely to succeed! Therein is the value of simulation.[25]

There are other serious issues that are of physical and social concern which are given special attention in the next section.

The Crisis in Health Care: Issues of Physical and Social Concern: Diabetes as a Prototype for Reform

Components of a Culture

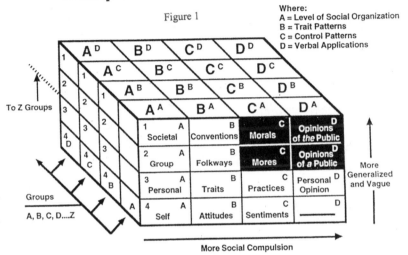

Figure 1

Where:
A = Level of Social Organization
B = Trait Patterns
C = Control Patterns
D = Verbal Applications

Adapted from The Shaping and Reshaping Forces of Acculturation: A Study of Risk, George Farrah © 1993, St. Coud, MN.

| 3C Practices |
| 4B Attitudes |

The health care industry has become a dominant factor in the American way of life. Reflecting the growing concern that the average citizen has for her/his health, the media has helped to shape this concern by featuring products and the results of research concerning a wide range of illnesses or diseases.[26] For example, in addition to information about cancer, both heart disease and diabetes have received special attention. Most important, in addition to stressing possible cures for these diseases, attention has been directed at the advantages offered by preventative and alternative medicine.

Since the health services system in our country has recently experienced dramatic changes especially new legislation involving the Medicare prescription policy, the emphasis in the medical profession is on cure. While most medical practices and hospital procedures are extremely efficient, there remains the critical issue of health care costs. Among the prominent diseases contributing to these rising medical costs, diabetes has reached the epidemic stage, particularly among children. Here, the attitudes regarding the amount and nutritional quality of the food consumed is of special importance to the general health of Americans.

For example, in the marketplace, one finds unique diets (i.e., low carbohydrates) and medications or other methods designed to help people reduce, such as stapling procedures. However, rather than cultivating the practices of employing a <u>regimen</u> which requires self-discipline, reliance is placed on a particular diet.[27]

Our doctors of internal medicine and general practitioners are acutely aware of the advantages of a regimen involving the value of regular exercise and the avoidance of excess sugar and fat and advise their patients accordingly. At the forefront of alternative medicine or complimentary healing (i.e., a combination of traditional medicine with avant-garde methods), is the well known physician, Dr. Andrew Weil. More than suggestions for losing weight, his medical ideas about health and well-being entail a neuro-psychological-immunological approach. With an international reputation, Dr. Weil has noted that nearly half of the U.S. adult population has used some form of alternative medicine, including herbs, traditional Chinese medicine, mind-body work, homeopathy and vitamin supplements.

Therefore, this radical departure from a reliance on the virtues of traditional medical practice really followed the nationwide trend and growing popularity of acceptance of alternative medicine. For example, reflecting the aforesaid opinion of Dr. Weil, during 1998, the Journal of the American Medical Association estimated that 42 percent of the Americans used one of 16 alternative therapies in 1997, an increase from 34 percent in 1990.[28] Without question, this departure from traditional medicine or the acceptance treatments, remedies or an emphasis on cure, is ample evidence that significant changes are occurring in the American way of health.

As an excellent barometer of these changes, one only has to follow the mass media and note the growing number of innovations, accounts, or testimonials given on behalf of a new awareness: that of preventative medicine.[29] In fact, one finds advertisements or booklets describing products from the distributors of vitamins and health products appearing periodically. Consider that the business generated from the sale of these products, ranging from a wide assortment of vitamins to an assortment of herbs, is most impressive. As it was recently reported in one of the popular health publications, Brian Carnahan, publisher of <u>Prevention</u> Health Books stated that:

> *"More than 60 million Americans—one third of our adult population—now use herbal remedies regularly. Consumers spent more than $12 <u>billion</u> last year (i.e., for the year 2000) on herbal and natural supplements alone. And business keeps getting better and better. That's great news, because herbs can work miracles of healing that no medicine can ever duplicate."[30]*

Fortunately, in the same article, Mr. Carnahan wisely cautions that "What you're not being told about buying and healing with herbal medicines, teas, supplements, and tinctures can render them useless—and even deadly."[31]

These cautions and issues noted above have also been echoed by many health professionals. Yet, via endorsements of sundry health products from national distributors of vitamins and herbs, nationally recognized medical doctors such as Andrew Weil and Julian Whitaker have written their own health letters that, for a small fee, are mailed periodically to their subscribers.[32] These and other comparable health letters from respected, widely recognized physicians contain valuable suggestions for a host of ailments. Therefore, this point of entry for providing medical advice or opinions on a variety of topics has become so pervasive that reputable medical authorities or even clinics have jumped on the bandwagon to claim their share of the marketplace! For example, during 2001, I received a cordial invitation from the desk of Robert D. Sheeler, M.D., the then Medical Editor of the Mayo Clinic Health Letter, inviting me to "preview an issue of America's most personal trustworthy health letter."

Quite clearly, Dr. Weil has assumed a strong leadership role in his advocacy of alternative and preventative medicine. For example, during the end of March, 2000, he was in Washington, D.C. in search of federal funds to incorporate the teaching of "integrated medicine" in all of America's medical schools. Here, it should be noted that, out of 125 medical schools in the United States, there are only three who are committed to this kind of training—these are 1) The University of Arizona; 2) The University of Minnesota; and 3) The University of Maryland.[33]

However, in the content analyses of the dominant themes or social issues contained in these excellent publications, the distinctions among or between the concepts of "cure" or "prevention," or "alternative medicine," or "spiritual healing," are blurred. No wonder that there is much confusion and uncertainty for so many Americans who are constantly deciding which advice or opinion is most helpful for their medical problems or ailments! Moreover, adding to this confusion, there is very little scientific evidence or research to buttress the claims made in so many publications concerning various aspects of healing.

Within the history of medical progress, we owe much to those creative thinkers who reshaped the future by seriously questioning time-honored traditions, institutions, and dogmas.

Consider the exciting sequence from William Harvey's (1578-1657) great discovery of how blood circulates in the human body to Madame Curie, Lister, Pasteur and other medical pioneers. Despite their contributions to an art with a scientific basis, during their creative days they were confronted with suspicion, doubt, or outright attacks—regardless of their proof which was obtained via first-hand observation, replication, or experimentation.

For example, in terms of first-hand observations and interviews, especially regarding the important role of "Medicines in Nature"— his title for the article—Joel L. Swerdlow, an Assistant Editor for the National Geographic magazine did a thorough analysis. In effect, he made personal visits to the forests of Madagascar, to India, and to the clay pits of Georgia. From these "hands-on" personal interactions or experiences with key individuals in the aforesaid geographic areas, he described various herbs or natural medicines relating to their curative or preventative value in the treatment of a number of diseases. However, in his excellent, penetrating account, Swerdlow was quick to note that not all of nature's plants are consistently reliable in their effectiveness as a cure. Yet, here, Arnold Relman, editor in chief emeritus of the New England Journal of Medicine, was quoted as stated that "many plant-derived materials have been proved to have important biological effects." Nevertheless, true to the rigorous standards of his profession and to the value of bona fide research methods, Dr. Relman advocates scientific testing and evaluation of any herbal remedies—despite their apparent ability to combat a wide range of illnesses.[34]

Nevertheless, the excellent record of medical practice and care in America owes its fine status to not only our dedicated health personnel, physicians, nurses, and support systems of persons, products, and processes, but also to the milestones of progress via research.

It is within the later context that our citizens and leadership can face the challenge and crisis posed by the health issue of diabetes. In this connection, I recently completed a three-year research project of this disease in our fifty states, including the District of Columbia.[35] The source of data came from the Centers of Disease Control and Prevention for the year 2000. Although these data did not differentiate between type I or type II diabetes, obesity and inactivity are regarded as vital factors in type II. In terms of this information, I am not certain of the samples or depth of the data which were collected for this purpose. One wonders: was their approach a micro model involving just a few numbers? Herein is a limitation for interpreting this research. Accordingly, the results from an analysis of several variables reflected the incidence of type II diabetes. These variables included 1) population; 2) housing units; 3) prevalence; 4) deaths; 5) geographic location; and   6) cost to each state.

For example, from an analyses of those variables, it was learned:

- That the relationship between the <u>prevalence of diabetes</u> in each state and its <u>individual population</u> was a significant one via the Pearson-Product-Moment method with an r = .000 for a 2-tailed test.

- That the states were ranked using a ratio of the percent of prevalence of diabetes to the state's percentage of the U.S. population.

- That the cost to states for diabetes amounted to a total of $158.2 billion. Among the states, the cost ranged from $.2 billion (Alaska) to $19.4 billion (California).

- That in terms of the percentage of the prevalence of diabetes exceeding the percentage of the population in a given state, there were 28 states with an index of one or more. Conversely, there were 23 states or 45 percent with a ratio of <u>less than one</u>. These included all 50 states plus the District of Columbia. Therefore, when the ratio is less or smaller than 1 the severity of diabetes in that particular state is relatively low. Conversely, when the ratio is greater or larger than 1, the severity of diabetes is relatively large.

- That an inspection of Tables 2 and 3 reveals an interesting geographic distribution of the prevalence of diabetes relating to the population in each state and the District of Columbia. For example, for those states east of the Mississippi River, with the exception of Maine, Vermont, New Hampshire, Georgia, and Virginia, the prevalence ratio was greater than 1.00. In a dramatic contrast, those states west of the Mississippi River, with the exception of Missouri, Arkansas, Louisiana, Oklahoma, California, and Oregon, the prevalence ratio was less than 1.00. One can only speculate as to why these latter differences in prevalence of diabetes exist. To what extent do one's lifestyle, eating habits, range and extent of activities (i.e., exercise, etc.) and the incidence of obesity contribute to this prevalence?

- That the maps of the United States illustrated in Figures 2 and 3, are related to the information provided in Tables 2 and 3 respectively. Most important, the states depict not only the geographic distribution, but also the severity of diabetes for each state. In effect, there is a dramatic contrast between the states east and west of the Mississippi River. Via these maps, one gains a better understanding and clearer picture of the same tabular information shown in Tables 2 and 3. The tables and figures may be found at the end of this chapter.

In conclusion, while there are many other issues of physical and social concern, diabetes is a prime example or prototype of the present crisis in health care. From a recent study, because

Table 2

Ratio of the Prevalence of Diabetes to the Population of Fifty States
and the District of Columbia

(Note: The data provided in the columns of Prevalence and Population are in percent)

State	Prevalence (Dividend)	Population (Divisor)	Ratio	Ratio + or -	Analysis
1. California	12.28	12.04	1.01	+	Analysis: Of 50 states plus the District of Columbia = 51
2. Texas	7.14	7.41	.96	-	
3. New York	6.90	6.74	1.02	+	
4. Florida	6.50	5.68	1.14	+	
5. Illinois	4.65	4.41	1.05	+	
6. Pennsylvania	4.85	4.36	1.11	+	1. Those states with 1 or more = 28 (55%)
7. Ohio	4.21	4.03	1.04	+	
8. Michigan	3.92	3.53	1.11	+	
9. New Jersey	2.86	2.99	.95	-	
10. Georgia	2.89	2.91	.99	-	2. Those states with less than 1 = 23 (45%)
11. North Carolina	3.04	2.86	1.06	+	
12. Virginia	2.41	2.52	.95	-	
13. Massachusetts	1.93	2.26	.85	-	
14. Indiana	2.27	2.16	1.05	+	
15. Washington	1.84	20.9	.88	-	
16. Tennessee	2.19	2.02	1.08	+	
17. Missouri	2.08	1.99	1.05	+	
18. Wisconsin	1.70	1.91	.89	-	
19. Maryland	2.00	1.88	1.06	+	
20. Arizona	1.26	1.82	.69	-	
21. Minnesota	1.39	1.75	.79	-	
22. Louisiana	1.66	1.59	1.04	+	

23. Alabama	1.96	1.58	1.24	+
24. Colorado	1.12	1.53	.73	-
25. Kentucky	1.51	1.44	1.04	+
26. South Carolina	1.52	1.43	1.06	+
27. Oklahoma	1.30	1.23	1.05	+
28. Oregon	1.10	1.22	1.72	+
29. Connecticut	.99	1.21	.81	-
30. Iowa	.98	1.04	.94	-
31. Mississippi	1.27	1.01	1.25	+
32. Kansas	.82	.96	.85	-
33. Arkansas	1.02	.95	1.07	+
34. Utah	.53	.79	.67	-
35. Nevada	.64	.71	.90	-
36. New Mexico	.58	.65	.89	-
37. West Virginia	.81	.64	1.26	+
38. Nebraska	.49	.61	.80	-
39. Idaho	.34	.46	.73	-
40. Maine	.39	.45	.86	-
41. New Hampshire	.31	.44	.70	-
42. Hawaii	.40	.43	.93	-
43. Rhode Island	.40	.37	1.08	+
44. Montana	.26	.32	.81	-
45. Delaware	.26	.28	.92	-
46. South Dakota	.20	.27	.74	-
47. North Dakota	.19	.23	.82	-
48. Alaska	.12	.22	.54	-
49. Vermont	.16	.22	.72	-
50. District of Columbia	.24	.20	1.20	+
51. Wyoming	.13	.18	.72	-

Table 3

Prevalence of Diabetes Versus the Population of Each Individual State and the District of Columbia

States Less than 1	Amount	States Greater than 1	Amount
1. Georgia	.99	1. West Virginia	1.26
2. Texas	.96	2. Mississippi	1.25
3. New Jersey	.95	3. Alabama	1.24
4. Virginia	.95	4. District of Columbia	1.20
5. Iowa	.94	5. Florida	1.14
6. Hawaii	.93	6. Pennsylvania	1.11
7. Delaware	.92	7. Michigan	1.11
8. Nevada	.90	8. Oregon	1.10
9. Wisconsin	.89	9. Tennessee	1.08
10. New Mexico	.89	10. Rhode Island	1.08
11. Washington	.88	11. Arkansas	1.07
12. Maine	.86	12. North Carolina	1.06
13. Massachusetts	.85	13. Maryland	1.06
14. Kansas	.85	14. South Carolina	1.06
15. North Dakota	.82	15. Illinois	1.05
16. Montana	.81	16. Missouri	1.05
17. Connecticut	.81	17. Indiana	1.05
18. Nebraska	.80	18. Oklahoma	1.05
19. Minnesota	.79	19. Kentucky	1.04
20. South Dakota	.74	20. Louisiana	1.04
21. Idaho	.73	21. Ohio	1.04
22. Colorado	.73	22. New York	1.02
23. Vermont	.72	23. California	1.01
24. Wyoming	.72		
25. New Hampshire	.70		
26. Arizona	.69		
27. Utah	.67		
28. Alaska	.54		

of inactivity and obesity, it was estimated that at least one in three Americans born in the year 2000 will develop diabetes at some stage in their lives. Of course, it should be noted that one in three people is not the same as one third of the United States population simply because not every person will develop diabetes at the same time.

Even in my own state of Minnesota, there is a growing public awareness of the rising prevalence and impact of this disease. In fact, it was recently reported by the Minnesota Department of Health officials that nearly 10 percent of Minnesota's population has diabetes or is at risk of acquiring it.

Finally, in terms of the prototype for the crises in health care, the issue of diabetes—especially type II—was given special attention. Ultimately, if we Americans are to cope successfully with this disease, the person who is afflicted or those who are on the borderline must assume the responsibility for its prevention by radical changes in their lifestyle or health habits.

Another critical issue in our way of life is the availability and reliability of transportation—both in rural and urban settings. It is considered next.

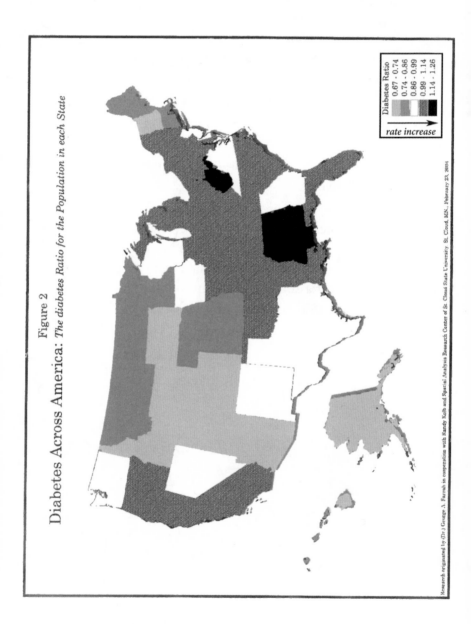

Figure 2
Diabetes Across America: *The diabetes Ratio for the Population in each State*

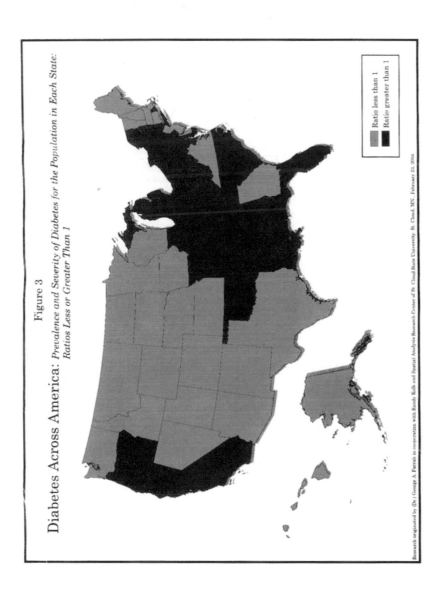

Figure 3

Diabetes Across America: *Prevalence and Severity of Diabetes for the Population in Each State: Ratios Less or Greater Than 1*

Ratio less than 1
Ratio greater than 1

Research originated by (Dr.) George A. Farrah in cooperation with Randy Kolb and Spatial Analysis Research Center of St. Cloud State University, St. Cloud, MN, February 23, 2004.

Transportation: Its Availability and Reliability

Components of a Culture

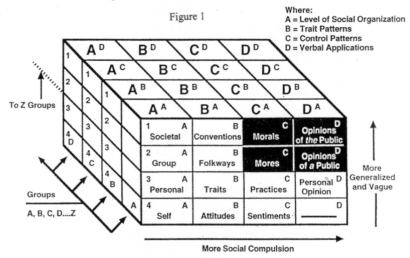

Figure 1

Where:
A = Level of Social Organization
B = Trait Patterns
C = Control Patterns
D = Verbal Applications

More Social Compulsion

Adapted from The Shaping and Reshaping Forces of Acculturation: A Study of Risk, George Farrah © 1993, St. Coud, MN.

3B Traits	3C Practices
4B Attitudes	4C Sentiments

Of all of the issues or concerns related to a deteriorating infrastructure in America, the issue of transportation deserves special attention. In terms of the components of a culture, the traits, attitudes, practices and sentiments of the choices we make are less generalized and vague. Therefore, these components are reflected and geared to needs on a personal level, as shown above, with the intervening traits, attitudes, practices, and sentiments. Here, choice does not mean a decision of "either/or," but, rather, working to achieve a much needed balance among several alternatives for travel. Accordingly, this section will focus on the need for alternative methods of travel rather than our heavy dependence on automobiles and airplanes. Trains and buses will also be given consideration.

While a thorough or in-depth analysis of the automobile and other means of transportation is beyond the scope of this book the automobile's contribution to our well-being as a society has been—and continues to be—highly significant! In retrospect, regarding its enormous impact, the milestones of its continuous and steady development can be briefly summarized below.

First, following the "horse and buggy" days of the nineteenth century, and the early years of the twentieth century, there was a growing number of automobiles on the roads of America during the 1920s.

Second, it was increasingly evident that the automobile affected a greater change in the American Way of Life than any other single cause up until the aforesaid time of the twenties.

Third, beginning in the 1920s as a relatively insignificant economic factor, by the time of the Great Depression during the thirties, it exceeded all other industries in its importance—even outranking the steel industry!

Fourth, innovations by the Ford Motor Company, General Motors, the Chrysler Corporation, and other manufacturers produced a <u>significant difference in the quantity and quality</u> of automobiles they produced. For examples, these great companies incorporated such manufacturing techniques as the standardization of interchangeable parts and mass production at a low cost. This progress by the companies involved made it possible for most American families to purchase an automobile of their preference.

Finally, the growth and development of the industry was utterly amazing: just imagine, by 1929, there were twenty-six and one-half million cars of various kinds registered![36] Then by the year 2000, the registration of all motor vehicles totaled 221,475,000, of which 133,621,000 were automobiles.[37] Compared to the registrations recorded for the year 1929, the increase was approximately sixty percent in just seventy one years![38] Consequently, this tremendous growth in the use of automobiles stimulated the building of more roads and highways. Its positive effect was to bring the country closer to the city, and, likewise the city to the country.

The wonderful and practical interstate system of highways that stretch in every direction across the United States enabled millions of Americans to begin new communities or suburbs away from large urban centers.[39] When, under President Eisenhower's administration, during the 1950's, the construction of freeways was begun, the federal government paid ninety percent while the states were responsible for only ten percent of the construction costs. This differential in payment is crucial when one considers the cost of maintaining this excellent network once the roads were completed. In fact, with the passage of time, there occurred an inversion of responsibility for payment of upkeep or improvement of new roads: the states now bear the major cost of repairs, improvements, or additions to existing routes.

With the passage of time, almost fifty years since the advent of the interstate system, the congestion in and around the large metropolitan areas has increased tremendously. Now that those who lived in the suburbs had to commute several miles from their homes or dwellings to their workplace, they depend heavily on their automobiles.

For those who depend on their automobiles for their transportation needs, the practice of traveling on roads and highways that have exceeded their capacity is disheartening.[40] No one enjoys waiting in traffic jams that occur with regularity during the morning and evening rush hours. In addition to this inconvenience, there are those drivers who ignore the posted speed limits and who drive at high speeds endangering their own safety as well as others. Herein, with this practice of disobeying the law—so prevalent or endemic on the roads and freeways across our country—there is the sentiment of cynicism. If articulated, the verbal sentiment would be expressed as "No way!" In other words, this driver feels that it is permissible to drive at any speed that fits the situation.

Fortunately, despite the pressures of time and congested highways, the majority of drivers are law abiding citizens. They relish their freedom and independence that the automobile provides. For the millions who use our great system of roadways, the reliability of the automobile—either made in American or manufactured elsewhere—has been more than satisfactory. Their reliability can be measured by the extended warranties now being offered by manufacturers, some that extend to five years—even to 100,000 miles.

Quite clearly, from the above analysis, the efficiency of the automobile is not in question. Rather, the problem resides in the limited choices that one has in order to travel for business or pleasure.

Without any doubt whatsoever, for the years ahead in the dawn of the twenty-first century, there will be many challenges facing the U.S. highway system, and we depend heavily on it. For example, it has been reported that our system presently handles ninety percent of all trips to and from work; it handles more than eighty percent of intercity-person trips over 100 miles; and finally, it handles seventy percent of freight traffic, based on billings.[41] More research is needed to further knowledge about highways in general and about their performance in particular. The amount of money spent on research is disappointing, because less than 0.6 percent of total highway expenditures is allocated for this purpose by highway agencies.[42]

Finally, with the daily and continuous use of our highways by millions of Americans, the renewal of United States highways should be a high priority item for the appropriate decision-makers. This task will require many years to accomplish; and the necessary funds, labor, and materials will be enormous. In particular, because we are so vitally dependent on our remarkable interstate highways, they must remain open to traffic while work is being done to reconstruct them. In order to accomplish the aforesaid task, careful planning must occur among those cities or communities involved, and who may be at odds in terms of their own objectives, means, ends, or other issues of disagreement. The principles involved in land use for additional highways must also include a better environmental balance as well as the social and economic considerations that such additions entail.

* *

Paralleling the tremendous surge of automobile transportation within the past fifty years, the airline industry has also flourished in America and elsewhere in the world. In effect, the major airlines have established reliable routes that connect cities via their system of "hubs," which are located in such cities as Detroit, MI and Charlotte, NC. When one considers the thousands of flight patterns and millions of passengers, the safety record of air travel is phenomenal!

Typical of all organizations, problems arise that threaten their very survival. For example, competition among the various airlines has been fierce, causing some to declare bankruptcy.[43] Even though airline deregulation has resulted in a general reduction of air fares—at least before the September 11th tragedy—the industry has been criticized for unfair competition.

There are other problems that have had a serious impact on a carrier's delivery system for its passengers. Contract negotiations involving service personnel such as mechanics, pilots, stewards, and stewardess have become longer and more contentious with the aforesaid personnel and their employers. For example, a few years ago, the ten-week-old strike by pilots of an affiliate carrier of Delta Air Lines shut down its regional jets.[44]

Yet, despite the escalating fuel costs; the ever-present threat of terrorist attacks; and, the problems noted above; our major airlines—an integral part of our economy and infrastructure—have made a remarkable effort to achieve some semblance of normalcy. Encouraged by the new emphasis on security concerning air travel, Americans are using the airlines again in increasing numbers. Most important, for leaders and other organizational/business personnel, the airplane offers the ultimate satisfaction in terms of speed and efficient service. In the competitive world of business, those in key positions know that their choice of air travel to accomplish a mission could make the difference between success and failure. What a positive difference this miracle of air travel has made in our lives!

* * * * * * * * * * * * * * * * * * ** * * * * * * *

The remainder of this section will focus on the train and bus as alternative methods of travel. At one time during the nineteenth century, the train was vital in the development of the western regions of the United States. Few lines were built before 1840, and our country had only 3,000 miles of tracks. However, just twenty years later, the nation had 30,000 miles of tracks, but most of it was in the Northeast. Then, by the year 1869, the first transcontinental railroad was an accomplished fact. The network of rail lines tied together vast sections of the American continent. Therefore, the railroads were a major instrument in the tremendous economic growth of America after the Civil War.

Resulting from the Panic of 1893, many railroads followed each other into receivership. For example, fifty six railroad companies were bankrupt: from the Erie; to the Union Pacific; and to the Northern Pacific.[45] Unfortunately, throughout its long, colorful, and productive history, the railroad industry has been confronted with very serious problems, not only because of financial setbacks, but also because of scandals and acquiring right-of-way space for its routes.[46]

In recent years, the alternative choice of transportation was provided by the Amtrak national system of trains. This system has achieved some degree of success, especially where there are heavily populated areas such as the northeastern corridor of our country. Unfortunately, in view of the latter exception and a few other profit making routes, the Amtrak system has not been profitable—despite its great potential.[47] Resembling somewhat the generous financial support given by several European countries to their railroads, our congress has continually allocated funding to avert a bankrupt Amtrak. This new and unusual "public debt" in transportation, which is quite common in some countries of Europe, particularly in Denmark and Germany, could be a realistic appraisal of our present system. In this connection concerning a public debt for transportation, when I was in the aforesaid countries on a research trip during the year 2000, I interviewed several leaders regarding the unequivocal financial support for their railroads. Their typical response really surprised me, and it took this form:

"Dr. Farrah, you wonder why we provide financial support for our railroads thereby creating a public debt. We do so because transportation, via railroads, is a way of life with us. Most important, this reliable way allows people of all ages to travel within and outside our country to their destination safely and on schedule, whether they are children or senior citizens."

He then continued, "While it is true that we have a public debt, millions of people in your country have private debts for their main transportation needs."

I retorted, "I really do not understand what kind of private debt to which you are referring. Could you please clarify that interesting comment?"

"Yes, of course," this leader replied. "The private debt is the money that people must repay a loan company or bank for their automobiles."

Ironically, in terms of Amtrak's public debt, William Jennings Bryant possessed the uncanny insight to understand this problem almost one hundred years ago. In effect, as a political candidate in the election of 1908, he advocated government ownership of railroads, not so much as an immediate issue, but as a long-range solution to its many problems. However, lacking the tradition, practice, and ethical commitment of the European countries regarding the transportation needs of its citizens, the political support for the present and future existence of Amtrak is dubious. According to an interview given by David Gunn, the Amtrak president and C.E.O, he commented on the "myth of self-sufficiency," and the politics involved which affect the future of Amtrak.

Rather than paint a portrait of gloom concerning our transportation needs, and, thanks to the attitude and spirit of "think how," or what was once known as "Yankee Ingenuity," innovations in many parts of America have resulted in significant changes. States such as New York, California, and Illinois—especially in the Chicago area—where there are great numbers of people, wisely developed and maintained alternative methods of travel for their citizens. For example, on the east coast, one can take the commuter rail which has routes and connections between cities in the region. In New York City, one can also use the subway or a boat to travel from one destination to another. California, too, boasts of a fine rail system that travels along the coast taking its passengers northward or southward, whatever the case may be. Then, in Chicago, in addition to numerous freeways, its citizens can resort to the elevated rail system or travel by commuter rail to reach their destinations. The ethical choices for the latter alternatives have been welcome exceptions to our great dependence on the automobile—particularly in the metropolitan areas.

As an image of the future, the prototype or example provided here is the Utah Transit Authority (i.e., UTA). For its innovations and achievements, in 2002, it was named "Transit System of the Year" by the American Public Transportation Association. The UTA received this signal honor because of its holistic approach in utilizing several features from its efficient organizational design. Organized around business units in neighboring cities, there are 38 light rail vehicles, 23 stations, and a total of 525 buses to supplement the rail lines. Other metropolitan areas have also made excellent progress in coping with traffic congestion by various kinds of innovations. These cities include Portland (Oregon); Atlanta; San Diego; San Francisco; and Washington, D.C. With its own unique innovation, the City of Indianapolis built a monorail or an elevated double rack guideway. The trains are fully automatic with onboard computer controls as well as a wireless data communications system.

Slowly but surely, states and municipal areas in many heavy populated locations have made rail based mass transit a high priority in planning for the future. The inclusion of buses is also an important item in their plans.

* *

Over the years, as a reliable means of transportation, the bus has provided a valuable service in the American way of life. Either publicly or privately owned, for short distance but in many instances for longer journeys across America, these excellent services continue to be a vital link in our transportation system.

Metro transit systems stand at the forefront in their efforts to provide efficient, reliable, and safe transportation at a reasonable fare. As a result, the majority—if not all—of the metropolitan areas in our country have made the choice of using buses for the key routes in their cities. Interestingly enough, departing from the gasoline or diesel operated bus, electric buses also have been utilized. In a partnership between the Metropolitan Transit District and the city of Santa Barbara, ten electric buses carry shoppers and tourists to the downtown business center and to the waterfront. For this innovative shuttle service, each bus is powered by over 100 batteries which last for eight hours.[48] Since many urban areas in California are concerned with the problem of pollution caused by motor vehicles using fossil fuels, the electric bus—or electric automobile for that matter—is a welcome alternative.

Hopefully such innovations will increase ridership in public transportation. If one compares the developments in bus transportation between Canada and the United States, especially since 1950, one discovers that Canada has been much more successful than we have in both increasing and maintaining ridership.[49] Yet, with imagination and a fine spirit of cooperation with existing metro transit systems, buses are now being utilized by universities in several metropolitan areas of our country. For example, in Salt Lake City, Utah, with the outstanding leadership provided by the Utah Transit Authority (UTA), a pass program was started for student use as a quid pro quo, both the UTA and the local university benefited from this splendid arrangement.[50]

In the case of our own Metropolitan Transit Commission in St. Cloud, and quite similar to the above arrangement, negotiated a free pass program with St. Cloud State University (SCSU).[51] As a favorable consequence which occurred in both universities described above, the shuttle systems for students—with efficient and reliable scheduling—reduced the need for more parking space on their campuses. However, SCSU still plans a parking facility on campus.

In summary, the components of culture relating to traits, attitudes, practices, and sentiments are important to the issues in transportation. The choices that our people make for their preference and method of travel have profound implications in terms of the fuel consumed and its effect on the environment. As Americans, we are extremely fortunate to have reliable and dependable means of transportation. Yet, even though the annihilation of distances via the great speed of airplanes—and lesser speeds by surface vehicles or trains—has had a tremendous impact on the socioeconomic life of America, our romance with automobiles continues unabated. To own your own automobile is a practice and sentiment deeply ingrained into American society.[52] Since all methods of travel are important at one time or another rather than pit the automobile or airplane against the alternative choices of inter-city trains, commuter, rail, light rail and buses, a balance must be achieved to maximize the efficiency and duration of our system of transportation; and to minimize the present stress on our highways. Without doubt, this matter of balance will be a thorny issue for leaders and decision-makers at all levels of government and the private sector in the years ahead.

* *

For the atomization of culture presented in Chapter 1, eight topics vital to the American Way of Life were analyzed as they related to the macro concept of our Western culture. Since the framework for this interpretation of culture involved sixteen components, each of the eight topics was intertwined with one or more of the components. Of these components, practices and sentiments were dominant themes in dramatic contrast to the glib and superficial use by so many persons—at all educational levels—in their flawed use of the word "culture." Therefore, the failure to address the identified sixteen components of our culture have atomized the components and weakened our vitality.

In Chapter 2, with the profound, and dynamic changes resulting from powerful shaping political, social and economic forces, an examination is given to these forces as the individual strives to give meaning to their existence.

Endnotes for Chapter 1

[1] The anthropological influence in the definition of culture and its distortion or misapplication was cited in the mid-1960's by Estelle Fuch's Pickets at the Gates. This reference was quoted by Eleanor Leacock in her article entitled, "Misapplication of the Culture Concept." She states "Such is often the case with the 'culture of poverty'" described by Fuch when this rendition of culture is carried to an extreme. Leacock concurs with Fuch in that, "Unfortunately, 'lower class culture' is fast becoming a new stereotype behind which the individual is not revealed more fully, but instead is lost" (my underlining here). This quote is from Francis A. J. Ianni and Edward Storey, Culture Relevance and Educational Issues (Boston: Little, Brown, and Company, Inc., 1973), p. 191.

[2] Op.. Cit., p. 193.

[3] The outstanding contributions of social psychologists or sociologists such as C. H. Cooley, G. H. Mead, and W. G. Sumner, all pioneers in their fields, were sources of knowledge, wisdom, and inspiration to me as an undergraduate and graduate student during my academic preparation at Wayne State University. Their ideas relating to important concepts as "group, folkways, mores, morals, societal, and practices" are vital to understanding these components of a culture—especially in a broader, macro view. In particular, see C. H. Cooley, Social Organization (New York: Charles Scribner and Sons, 1909); G. H. Mead, Mind, Self, and Society (University of Chicago Press, 1934); and W. G. Sumner, Folkways: A Study of the Sociological Importance of Usages, Manners, Customs, Mores, and Morals (New York: Ginn and Company, 1940).

[4] It was Adam Smith, who, in 1759, provided a comprehensive rationale for the concept of sentiments by writing The Theory of Moral Sentiments. Of special significance was the emphasis he placed on "propriety" and the "amiable and respectable virtues" cast within the framework of action. Then seventeen years later, he wrote The Wealth of Nations. Quite clearly, any critic of this work should read

the former book first before rendering judgment of his ideas put forth in the second work. For better understanding of Smith's ideas about virtues, see The Theory of Moral Sentiments (New York: Augustus M. Kelly, 1966), pp. 26-51.

[5] An attitude may be defined as not only a manner of acting, feeling, or thinking that shows one's disposition or opinion regarding an issue, but, it is also the tendency to react in a certain way—even though the reaction does not take place!

[6] See B. J. Hodge and William P. Anthony, Organizational Theory (Boston: Allyn and Bacon, 1979). Interestingly enough, in this first edition, culture was defined as "The sum total of learned behavior traits characteristic of the members of a society; the values, norms, artifacts, and accepted behavior patterns of a society." However, in a revised Fourth Edition of 1984, the definition was modified by the addition of a Chapter 13, entitled "Organizational Culture" which included "thick and thin cultures" found in workplaces such as the Ford Motor Company (i.e., in this case, a "thick culture"; see p. 448).

[7] During 1976, he was teaching a class at the University of Minnesota entitled, "Teaching the American Indian Student." It should be noted that his definition does not fall into the trap of cultural relativism which atomizes culture. Closely related to the latter definition is the fascinating, detailed account of the acculturation process in Western history authored by R. Freeman Butts. See, for example, his text entitled, A Cultural History of Education (New York: McGraw-Hill Book Co., 1947). As in the case of Dr. Butts, nowhere in the definition by Chuck Robinson does one find a misapplication of culture with adjectives such as "thick" or "thin culture." It is really remarkable that an indigenous American provides a definition of culture quite similar to the European-American version despite other differences.

[8] Ibid.

[9] In addition to John Dewey's contributions in the discipline of philosophy and psychology, he left a lasting legacy in education. His ideas, centering on the dominant theme of "The School as a Special Environment," were designed for the growth of intelligence. His text, Democracy and Education (New York, NY: Macmillan Co.,

1916) contains a wealth of information, especially his chapter on the philosophy of education, pp. 22-24.

[10] As a veteran of World War II, with 31 months overseas in four campaigns with the Southwest Pacific Forces of General Douglas MacArthur, I understand the commitment of our splendid troops in Iraq and elsewhere.

[11] With the passage of time, it is increasingly becoming evident that the information regarding the war in Iraq supplied by our political leadership and/or agencies has been flawed.

[12] In passing, it is interesting to note the project currently underway at St. John's University, located a short distance from St. Cloud, MN. Funded by a research grant and with the leadership of an expert from England, a Holy Bible is being hand-written and illustrated in color— similar to the works of those gifted monks of another, earlier era!

[13] These dialogues were in the form of interviews which I conducted in Germany and Switzerland during a sabbatical leave in 1982.

[14] During the late 1990's, a pilot study involving the use of a computer in reading instruction was conducted at the elementary schools of Duluth, MN. As a Title I grant award, a comparison was made between two groups. In one group, mentors were used with students using computer assisted instruction while the other group of students did not have mentors in their use of the same computer assisted instruction. Without question, the process of interaction enhanced the group of students who had mentors.

[15] In general, a convention is defined as an agreement between persons on the uses and practices of behavior, especially in social life.

[16] For example, Robert Bellah et al. state that "however much Americans extol the autonomy and self-reliance of the individual, they do not imagine that a good life can be lived alone. Those we interviewed would almost all agree that connectedness to others in work, love, and community is essential to happiness, self-esteem, and moral worth." See their work: Habits of the Heart (New York: Harper and Row, Publishers, 1985), pp. 90-93.

[17] Ibid.

[18] For additional information dealing with the subject of marriage, see Patrick J. Buchanan, The Death of the West (New York: Thomas Dunne Books, 2002), pp. 42-43.

[19] For an excellent treatment of the development of personality, see Personality and Problems of Adjustment (New York: F. S. Crofts & Co., 1947), 868pp.

[20] In his pioneer work while a professor of political and social science at Yale University, Dr. William Graham Sumner provided dynamic applications of the mores in his brilliant book of Folkways.

[21] It has been reported that "since the North American Free Trade Agreement (NAFTA) took effect in 1994, more than 700,000 U.S. jobs have disappeared as scores of employers move to take advantage of low wages and a lax regulatory environment south of the border." For example, Electrolux, a multibillion dollar Swedish firm that is the world's largest maker of power appliances, intends to close its Greenville, Michigan refrigerator plant in order to relocate in Mexico. As a result, 2700 people there will lose their jobs. This Stockholm-based company employs 1800 people in my own city of St. Cloud—its only North American freezer plant. Being one of St. Cloud's largest employers, it manufactures 2 million freezers a year; but it now faces the same closure as the Greenville, MI plant. This information was extracted from an article by Ron Gettelfinger which appeared in the St. Cloud (MN) Times of Sunday, February 8, 2004, p. 7B.

[22] For a more intensive examination of this division of power, see Chapter 4.

[23] Charles A. Beard and Mary R. Beard, America in Midpassage (New York: The Macmillan Co., 1939), 500 pp.

[24] A. Toynbee, A Study of History (New York: Oxford University Press, 1947), an abridgment of Volumes I-VI by D.C. Somervell.

[25] During the academic years of 1973-74, I was selected to direct the very first international program in Europe which involved over 100 university students and 12 professors for the above academic year. Since our classes were held in a study center located in Fredericia, one of the classes I taught involved methods of planning. I invited Danish leaders from government and business to share their methods with our students.

[26] Several television channels now feature special reports on various diseases. In particular, WCCO of the Twin Cities area, is an affiliate of

the C.B.S. network and it is currently (i.e., February, 2004) featuring heart disease in women.

[27] When shopping for food at the supermarket or grocery store, one now finds an emphasis on low-carbohydrate foods of all varieties which is based on the Atkins diet. In effect, rather than a balanced choice of nutrients, the obese person is allowed to indulge in as much fatty or high protein food as he/she desires in order to lose weight.

[28] See November 11, 1998 issue of their Journal for the article entitled "Trends in Alternative Medicine Use in the United States: Results of a Follow-up National Survey," pp. 1569-1575. Chicago, IL: American Medical Association.

[29] Across America, via newspapers, radio, television, magazines, and periodicals, one can read accounts or various viewpoints concerning preventative medicine.

[30] From Prevention Magazines' Special Consumer Edition, March 2000, Emmaus, PA: Prevention Health Books.

[31] Ibid.

[32] Dr. Weil's health letter is entitled "Self-Healing: Creating Natural Health for Your Body and Mind," published at 42 Pleasant Street, Watertown, MA.

[33] From the March 31, 2000 issue of The Arizona Daily Star, p. 6, sec. B.

[34] For the complete article by Swerdlow, see the National Geographic issue for April 2000, pp. 98-117. Official Journal of the National Geographic Society.

[35] See Tables 1 and 2 for these analyses. See also Figures A and B for colorful maps depicting the prevalence and severity of diabetes among the 50 states and the District of Columbia.

[36] Extracted from John D. Hicks, The American Nation (Boston: Houghton Mifflin Co., 1946), p. 617.

[37] U. S. Census Bureau, No. 1062, State Motor Vehicle Registrations: 1980 to 2000—Transportation (Washington, DC, 2000), p. 674.

[38] Ibid.

[39] For an excellent treatment of the problems confronting the U.S. highway system, see the article by Robert E. Skinner, "Highway

Research for the 21ˢᵗ Century," Issues in Science and Technology, Vol. 19, no. 2 (Winter 2002/2003), pp. 31-35.

[40] Ibid.

[41] Robert E. Skinner, op. cit., pp. 31-35.

[42] Ibid.

[43] For example, because Delta Airlines has lost $3.2 billion in the past three years following the September 11 terrorist attacks, there is a growing fear among Delta employees of an eventual Chapter 11 filing. Reported in USA Today, Section B of the Thursday, March 18, 2004 edition.

[44] See "Conair Strike Casts a Long Shadow," by James Ott, in Aviation Week and Space Technology, Vol. 154, no. 23 (June 4, 2001, pp. 47-49. To this very day (i.e., March 22, 2004), Delta Airlines, as other major airlines, continue to face serious financial problems.

[45] John D. Hicks, op cit., p. 255.

[46] Ibid., p. 75.

[47] During an interview, David Gunn, the Amtrak president and C.E.O., made several observations about Amtrak's credibility, the "myth of self-sufficiency," and Washington politics which affect the future of Amtrak. This information was extracted from Mass Transit, vol. 29, no. 8 (2003), 16 (10 pages).

[48] This article, entitled "Downtown Shuttle Hits Milestone," appeared in the publication American City and Country, vol. 115, no. 3 (February 2000), p. 53. The author is anonymous.

[49] John Pucher, "Public Transport Developments: Canada vs the United States," Transportation Quarterly, Vol. 48, no. 1 (Winter 1994), pp. 65-78.

[50] Jim Duffy, Mass Transit, Vol. 29, issue 6 (Sept-Oct 2003), p. 24. The university is very pleased with the student pass program and their cooperative efforts with the Utah Transit Authority.

[51] In an interview with Thomas Cruikshank, Director of Planning for the St. Cloud Metropolitan Transit Commission (MTC), I learned that the free pass program for SCSU has dramatically increased student ridership. For example, for all city routes involving bus routes strictly for student use, the yield of passengers increased from a February 2003 total of 148,531 to a February 2004 total of 73,287—an increase of

24,756. Later, I verified the aforesaid information with Steve Ludwig, Vice-President of Administrative Affairs and the contact or liaison person with the MTC of St. Cloud. He agreed that the free pass system for students has been a great success. For an assessment of student satisfaction of the program, an "MTC Ridership Survey" was conducted during November of 2003. In terms of key items regarding overall satisfaction, the responses from those students involved a high level of satisfaction.

[52] This sentiment was expressed by Thomas Cruikshank in the above interview.

CHAPTER TWO

NEW STRIVINGS FOR MEANING AND IDENTITY

Three Aspects of Personality and Related Values

Components of a Culture

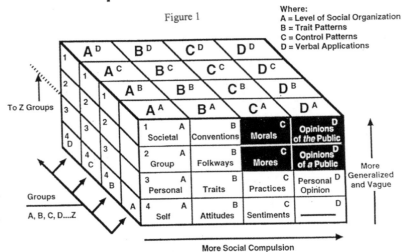

Figure 1

Where:
A = Level of Social Organization
B = Trait Patterns
C = Control Patterns
D = Verbal Applications

Adapted from The Shaping and Reshaping Forces of Acculturation: A Study of Risk, George Farrah © 1993, St. Coud, MN.

3B Traits
4B Attitudes

Without question, the shaping force of psychology has been a dominant characteristic of the past century. I believe that with the passage of time, just as the Eighteenth Century has become known as "The Century of Rationalism," and the Nineteenth as "The Century of Nationalism," the Twentieth will become known as "The Century of Psychology." At great risk of oversimplification, the treatment here of the aforesaid three aspects of personality and values relate directly to my numerous research projects. It is from these validated projects that I characterized the three aspects as coping, interacting, and applying. These are the behavioral patterns observed from the cultural components extracted from the above figure in column B. It should also be noted that the Traits and Attitudes tend to be <u>less</u> generalized and vague.

As an approach to understanding the dynamic process of human behavior, the practice of psychology actually has its historical roots in the field of philosophy. Before the Twentieth Century and the work of pioneers in this nascent discipline, the term "psychology" was not known in the specialized way as it is known today. Rather, for matters or considerations of mental qualities, it was left to the philosophers to appraise or evaluate.

Since the concept of trait describes a distinguishing quality or characteristic of the personality, it plays a significant role in how the individual copes, interacts, and, applies in any given situation with values as a directional compass point. As this particular section unfolds, the relationship between the three aspects of personality and the values will be described.

The concept of attitude–resting at the lowest level of cultural components–has often been misused in describing changes of behavior. If an attitude is defined as a tendency to react (or interact) in a certain manner even though the reaction does not take place, then caution must be exercised regarding changes of behavior. Therefore, what is commonly referred to as "attitude"– a much deeper aspect of personality–is really an opinion, which is more subject to change than the aforesaid attitude.

In retrospect, for nearly a century, the study of personality has become a growing practice. In fact, the two pioneers of psychoanalysis, Sigmund Freud and Carl G. Jung formed a historic friendship shortly after they met in 1907. As Jung worked under the medical guidance of Freud, he observed that in the course of development, individuals begin to adopt habitual attitudes which determine how they experience life. Unfortunately, as Jung continued to work with his mentor, Freud, the two began to experience great differences in their interpretation of both theory and practice. Eventually, this conflict and separation became known as "years of friendship, years of loss."[1]

Yet, it was Jung who not only categorized personality types, but he also provided a rationale for a better understanding of values. His rationale involved the concepts of shaping and reshaping which are really the catalytic agents in the transformation of values. The historical antecedents for these latter ideas may be found in the literary works of Johann W. Goethe. It was in German that Goethe wrote, "Gestaltung, Umgestaltung, Das ew'gen, 'Sinnes, ew'ge Unterhaltung" (i.e., Shaping-reshaping: The eternal spirit's eternal pastime."[2] Quite clearly, as Goethe and Jung, poet and psychiatrist respectively, observed, the concepts of shaping and reshaping are not new by any means!

In my usage here and elsewhere, shaping refers to the external forces which converge on the individual, forces over which the individual has little or no control. For example, these forces which shape the individual emanate from the macro or micro environments of cultural aspects, political, economic, social, religious, educational, government, or mass media sources of influence.[3] Therefore, these shaping forces, as it were, "sets the stage" for the formation of the individual's value system.[4]

Conversely, reshaping involves the individual's response or reaction to these sources of influence. The response may be immediate or latent. For example, if the shaping forces come from the schools, then this influence is latent because of the delayed maturation process. Of course, the nature of the response is dynamically and reciprocally related to the individual's perception of the shaping values.

Suppose, for instance, that the shaping forces happen to come from the mass media (i.e., where, as described in an earlier section, there is often distortion in meaning), how does the individual transform that data or information so that he or she can reshape the phenomena for meaning to him or her? In addition, there are also the various, obvious distortions that come from political leaders who use the mass media or advertising in their campaigns for shaping public opinions and choices of their constituents. Thus, it is also crucial for the person involved in the activities of everyday living to have the abilities and skills that are inherent in coping.

The remainder of this section provides crucial knowledge gleaned from my extended research abroad from my European samples and from sampling persons in our own country. In effect, as a result of extensive statistical analysis featuring factor analysis, I discovered nine values that became operational in how one copes, interacts, and applies skills or abilities.

From this longitudinal research, a set of nine basic values emerged as "the most significant" to those individuals who participated.[5]   This set of values was evident regardless of educational level, work choice, age, gender, and location. These related values to the aforesaid three aspects of personality involved: 1) success; 2) Self-confidence and being understood; 3) Reaction to failure; 4) Coping with change; 5) Experiencing the new or different; 6) Service, honesty, and helping others; 7) Coping with self-doubt; 8) Understanding the application of knowledge; and, 9) The work ethic.

Knowledge and familiarity with this set of values has proved to be extremely beneficial to a number of different groups including students (i.e., from the middle school level to graduate school), counselors, parents, administrators as well as business and government leaders. From various evaluation reports or analyses of data respondents indicated that these values were fundamental to the development of a sense of responsibility–especially within the reshaping mechanism of one's inner-directionedness.

Despite ample evidence that America is now an aging population, societal emphasis has been directed to the advantages of youth. Since age is a crucial variable in achieving status via economic and social advancement, one's age is intimately associated with success and failure.

There are also pressures on the individual to reach goals as quickly as possible. Consequently, the shaping on external forces–given impetus by the mass media or general advertising– stress <u>immediate satisfaction</u>, and one's choices are based on this time element! However, many worthwhile goals are <u>latent</u> in nature, springing forth from internal factors or the qualities of inner-directedness. In effect, these goals may take years of hard work–of coping, interacting, and applying skills–to realize, often extending beyond the age of forty.

The values of experiencing something new or different are characteristic of the individuals who change from job to job during their career in hopes of realizing one or more goals. Usually, if the goal involved is a professional one, then many years of devoted study, often involving the attainment of a degree, may be necessary. Increasingly, one finds older persons, as "non-traditional students," returning to institutions of higher learning in order to advance their learning.

Finally, regardless of gender, age, or location, the attributes of success or failure are dynamically related to how one copes, interacts, or applies the required skills and knowledge in any given situation. As shown in Figure 4, there is a dichotomy between the qualities that are immediate-intrinsic in contrast to those which are latent: the fulfillment-extrinsic qualities. Whether the person is in school; higher education; or employed in a particular job or profession, the qualities of competition, tasks/projects, discovery/creativity are of the immediate-intrinsic variety.

Conversely, those qualities featuring the fulfillment-extrinsic domain are aspiration, cooperation, conformity, responsibility, and acceptance-praise. As noted earlier, there is considerable overlap between the latter two domains as well a the ability to cope, interact, or apply.

In their professional work, psychologists have been acutely aware of these three aspects of personality presented here. However, their concern and efforts are usually directed to the abnormal traits or attitudes revealed in therapy sessions by their patients rather than a more normalized population. Without doubt, the two cultural components of traits and attitudes are intimately related to the strivings for one's existential meaning and identity.

Significantly, over the years, several Minnesota school districts utilized curriculum designs which included the nine values. Via problem-solving situations, teachers or professors were able to incorporate the three aspects of personality (i.e., coping, interacting and applying) with the nine values. Students have benefited from problem-solving episodes in which they become aware of the clear relationship of what they were asked to do in terms of their own goals—which were often prioritized in their order of importance. Both goal attainment and personal investment were enhanced because students were able to participate in planning, decision making, and self-evaluation.

This "think-how" process supplemented the more traditional "know-how," where flexibility of choice and alternative learning styles have been limited. Assuredly, not only those students who participated in the latter school districts, but also the graduate students I taught at several military bases and adhered to the worth of the nine values gained from their efforts.[6] Conversely, those who did not, were at-risk academically.

Specifically, these nine values became operational in the forms of coping, interacting with others, and applying knowledge and skills in real-life situations. As shown in Figure 4, these forms of reshaping characteristics are related and can be traced to items contained in surveys for various academic levels, from middle school to graduate level work.

Figure 4

The Three Aspects of Personality

Key To Symbols
Immediate-Intrinsic **versus** Fulfillment-Extrinsic

A. Evaluated Competition	e. Aspiration
B. Tasks/Projects	f. Cooperation/Conformity
C. Discovery/Creativity	g. Responsibility
D. Skills	h. Acceptance/Praise

Items In Each Category   Total

						Total
I. Coping Skills	A=5	C=2	D=1	g=1	h=1	(10)
II. Interacting Skills	B=1	C=1	e=1	g=1	h=3	(7)
III. Applying Skills	B=2	D=1	e=3	f=1		(7)
					Total=	(24)

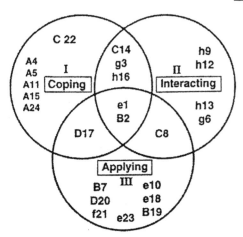

. From this portrayal of the three aspects of personality, one observes that there is considerable overlap between coping, interacting and applying.[7] In its survey form, the first aspect of coping has the largest cluster of items. These items indicate how a person copes with success, failure, change, experiencing something new or different, and self-doubt in his/her life. In a world and nation full of uncertainty and ambiguity stemming from many shaping forces (i.e., government, economics, mass media, cultural aspects, education, technology, and religion) so many individuals may find it difficult or simply intolerable to cope with these forces.

The consequences of the inability of our citizens to cope with these shaping forces–especially the impact resulting from change, failure, self-doubt, or circumstances beyond their control–can put these persons at risk. As a consequence, the summative effect weakens cultural vitality or practices at all levels; from the local community; to the state; and to our nation.

Therefore, the loss of cultural vitality associated with the inability to cope, interact, and apply within our democratic process is strongly related to the atomization of culture. Finally, the aforesaid inability to apply much needed solutions to vital problems leads to serious crises in health care, transportation, government, and other services or agencies in our American Way of Life.

Since matters of faith provide meaning and spiritual identity for the individual, dynamic changes have occurred in orthodoxy. Yet, the apparent need for a belief system is common and necessary wherever the faithful worship. Accordingly, its strengths and weaknesses are considered in the section that follows.

Changes in Orthodoxy: Its Vitality and Anemia

Components of a Culture

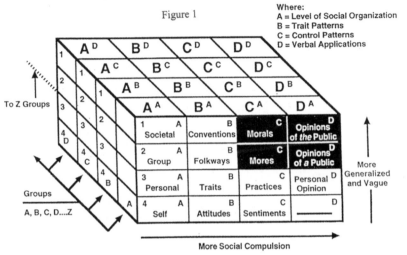

Figure 1

Where:
A = Level of Social Organization
B = Trait Patterns
C = Control Patterns
D = Verbal Applications

Adapted from *The Shaping and Reshaping Forces of Acculturation: A Study of Risk*, George Farrah © 1993, St. Coud, MN.

| | All Components Are Involved | |

Since the Western world has many images or variations of Christianity, its dominant orthodoxy, there have been many significant changes over the centuries. In this section, it is not my intent to examine the continual process of reform and internal pluralism that characterizes this faith. The worldwide religious diversity is reflected in the over four hundred denominations which all identify themselves as Christians.[8] Rather, special attention will be directed to certain aspects of the church–regardless of its denomination–in terms of its weaknesses and strengths.

However in terms of the components of a culture, although all components are interwoven in this instance of orthodoxy, within column C of the above figure, there is a gulf or distance between our morals and mores in the American Way of Life. For the spiritual thoughts or ideas of what "Should Be," this gulf is evident in the "Mores," or the immediately apprehended action or behavior of the person, the "Is." It is the lack of agreement between these two cultural components that helps to contribute to our loss of cultural vitality.

Again, in this same column C, the religious practices and sentiments reflect the distance that exists between the morals and mores. In turn, the conventions, folkways, traits, and attitudes which are evident in column B, influence the mores–those ways of thinking, feeling, and acting that are necessary for a group to survive.

Within the many faiths of mankind, from the Abrahamic Faiths (i.e., Judaism, Christianity, and Islam), to the Vedic Faiths and others such as Shinto, Taoism, etc., each has a plan for facing challenges of the present and the future.[9] With their different beliefs, heresies, and moral laws, their founding prophets, visionaries, and messiahs share an amazing similarity in their approach to salvation. For example, the above components of a culture have applicability not only to Christianity but to all major belief systems. It is the reason why all of the above components are woven into the fabric of every major religion. Some of that fabric may be worn out but it remains useable and fashionable for one to wear–even with its shabby appearance.

However, having only a limited knowledge of the many religions in our world, my intent in this section is not to make a comparative analysis of these faiths, nor is it my purpose to judge the worth of these belief systems because they are truly portraits in spiritual diversity. Accordingly, the choices which individuals make in their individual cultural settings are guides for their moral conduct and behavior.

As a practicing Christian, my observations for this section are the results of interviews with several individuals–both men and women–who are well versed in the Christian faith. In terms of their denominations, they represent the Orthodox, Catholic, and Protestant faiths. The generalizations which follow were based on this one question: As a leader in your particular church, what do you believe to be its strengths and weaknesses? The responses that I obtained from these six church leaders have been recast into the following generalizations which reflect the gap between our morals and our mores.

First, in terms of the vitality of our Christian faith, these dominant themes, expressed by all who participated, emerged:

- That for over 2,000 years, despite internal strife and dissentions, the message of Jesus and His disciples remains strong.

- That His divinity and resurrection provide hope for eternal life.

- That for Christians, faith in God is faith in the invisible.

- That this faith has the characteristic of being latent, or future oriented, which is in contrast to faith in the visible or the immediately apprehended. For example, when questioned, our Lord, Jesus replied, "My kingdom is not of this world."

- That with this latent faith as a moral compass, one's behavior toward others is guided by the values and sentiments of compassion, forgiveness, charity, and hope to become a better person, and thus avoid sinful behavior.[10]

- That with this Christian faith, other forms or variations of faith are also applicable in our daily lives. For example, one can have faith in family life; faith in others; faith in the future; faith in the workplace; faith in leadership; and this list can be extended and applied to myriad situations or conditions.

Without a doubt, with a larger sample from which responses could be extracted from the aforesaid question, more generalizations, just as valid as those which I recast, could also be obtained from other leaders. Most important, as our faith is enhanced, the gap between what "Should Be" (i.e., Our Morals) and the "What Is" (i.e., Our Mores) lessens considerably. When there is less distance between these vital cultural components, especially in terms of the person's daily behavior, the personality of this person becomes more integrated. In effect, because of a purity of purpose and affirmation of the value, the actualization of the idea into a positive act of being of service or helping another person contributes to our cultural vitality. Regardless of religious preference, within the macro environment, these spiritual choices—especially honesty, helping others, or being of service to the sick or poor—can make a significant difference in our American Way of Life. Herein, is one small portrait of our religious faith and strength.

My second consideration for this particular section concerns the anemia or weaknesses of our Christian faith.[11] Again, from the dominant themes provided by those church leaders who I interviewed, it is quite clear that changes in our orthodoxy have contributed to the anemia. These generalizations resulting from analysis of their responses are apparent.

- That as an Orthodox leader expressed it, without unity there is little strength and a sense of community is almost impossible to achieve.[12] For example, in Greece and in Orthodox towns in Cyprus, Christianity defines, guides, and strengthens the community.[13] People there do not have to hide their faith under a bushel basket, nor stutter at Christmas and Easter! Thus, there is little distance between the morals and mores.

- That even though the religious base of Europe and the Americas is Christianity, one discovers that editors of major journals and institutions created by Christians are too timid even to use the symbols B.C. and A.D. in dating historical events!

- That the social revolution of the 1960s ushered into religious practice belief prayers, creeds (i.e., the "Book of Order"; "From a Brief Statement of Faith"), or other excerpts selected by the minister. Most important, as an affirmation of Faith— a traditional portion of the Sunday worship service, these supplementary choices were used in place of the Apostles Creed. While the Apostles Creed remains an integral part of the Catholic and Orthodox Service, Protestant churches have not been consistent in having it as a part of their worship service. In view of the fact that it has been over 2,000 years since the biblical teaching of Jesus and his disciples, there is constantly the possibility that His teachings will be changed, distorted or ignored with the passage of time and the pressures to change.

- That symptomatic of the problems we face as a larger church is the fact that seminary enrollment is down significantly in all main line denominations. For example, in the Presbyterian Church, as of a recent report, the number of pastors has declined by seventeen percent since 1985. Then, according to the PC-USA (i.e., Presbyterian Church of the United States of America) Research Services, there are over 2,000 churches looking for some kind of ministerial leadership. Therefore, as the spiritual element of dedicated ministers grows less in number, this shortage will eventually affect the lifeblood of the local church—its membership.

* * * * * * * * * * * * * * * * *

In summary, the points of tension that exist between the conditions of vitality and those of anemia must be erased if Christianity is to produce a positive difference in the lives of people. As shown in column D of the Components of a Culture, the verbal applications relating to "Opinions of a Public" can be applied to any religious denomination. For example, these latter opinions as well as the "Personal Opinions" below it (i.e., in the "Components of a Culture" illustration) are also expressed as matters of principles of faith. At these levels, there is more social compulsion to conform. Whenever there is a loss of membership or a drop in attendance in a particular church—for whatever reason—the dissatisfaction, via the expression of opinions among the congregation, travels like wildfire! When people leave a church in order to find a spiritual home more to their satisfaction, it is really not possible for them to have inner peace and a harmonious community of believers when basic ideals of its members contradict each other.

Within the shaping forces that affect the components of a culture, the art of persuasion is a significant factor in our practices and sentiments. Its impact is considered in the following section.

Masters of Dread: The Art of Persuasion

Components of a Culture

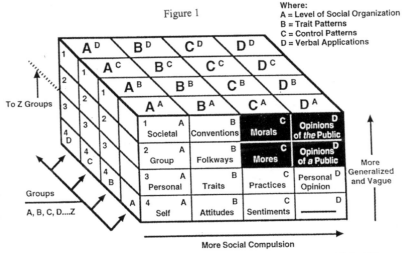

Figure 1

Where:
A = Level of Social Organization
B = Trait Patterns
C = Control Patterns
D = Verbal Applications

Adapted from The Shaping and Reshaping Forces of Acculturation: A Study of Risk, George Farrah © 1993, St. Coud, MN.

3C Practices	1D Opinions of a Public
4C Sentiments	3D Personal Opinion

As described earlier in Chapter 1, the shaping forces of mass media and articulate propaganda are vital as one strives for meaning and identity.[14] Political leaders or members of congress are adept in the art of persuasion in order to promote a particular issue or their personal agenda. Their personal opinions regarding an issue may not reflect the opinions of a public, and their views may be at odds with that public.[15]

For example, at this writing, there are two issues—among many—that have caused considerable disagreement among our legislative representatives and their constituents. The first, related to the graying of America and the "Baby Boomers," concerned with the solvency and future of social security.

As thousands of Americans reach or contemplate retirement, they have been bombarded with the polemics of a grim outlook of future benefits from social security. Is it any wonder that these citizens, exposed to the drumbeat—repeated over and over again—of a failed system of financial security as they age, experience the feeling of dread? However, our many publics, members of an alarming, shrinking middle class feel or express sentiments and personal opinions contrary to what they are led to believe. Of course, with our involvement of a war in Iraq and political tensions elsewhere in the Middle East, the financial cost is in the billions and it continues to grow unabated! Therefore, our priorities have shifted and the social effects are evident at all levels of government—especially those needed programs to assist the less fortunate or disenfranchised persons in our sprawling inner urban cities or rural areas of America.

Most advanced countries, especially those in Europe, have some form of what we characterize as "Social Security." For example, while in Goteborg, Sweden, it was my good fortune to interview a lawyer regarding their economic priorities and the choices that are made by their political leaders.[16] When I asked him his opinion regarding the retirement benefits for those who choose to retire, he replied that they receive a pension from the government. He explained that to support this pension plan, their taxing structure or plan was "the middle way," where the wealthier class of citizens bore the brunt. As a result, there were fewer very rich and fewer very poor—thus creating a more equitable effect which resulted in "the middle way."

Quite clearly, this ethical imperative of ensuring that a nation's older citizens can live their retirement years in dignity and the relative comfort of economic security is a worthy goal to achieve. Here, in our truly blessed and prosperous America, since the leadership of President Franklin D. Roosevelt, from the 1930's to the present day, social security has helped to provide a measure of economic security for millions of Americans, and that goal was achieved. However, the current national leadership would privatize social security, scuttle a reliable trust fund—much like "borrowing from Peter to pay Paul"—a fund that has been diminished by transferring money to a general fund; and then promote speculation of citizen's savings in a fickle and uncertain market place. The prophets of doom have distorted the advantages of a stable and reliable system in favor of gambling on a questionable alternative fraught with risk. However, when it comes to our leadership crying out against the pervasive greed that has seized our wonderful country, there is only silence![17]

The second issue involves the shabby treatment given to our veterans by members of our Congress. For many years, the pressing needs of sick and disabled veterans have not been met. For example, the discretionary funding method, which is presently used, is woefully inadequate. As this method continues, and as health care costs rise, there is also an increased demand for medical services. To further confound this desperate situation, Congress has not been able to complete the vital appropriations process on time. This delay profoundly affects the Department of Veterans Affairs (i.e., VA) medical care services at its many excellent centers throughout our country.[18]

In retrospect, it is important to recall the positions taken by the two presidential candidates in the recent 2004 election. Really, in terms of their responses given during interviews with the Disabled American Veterans (i.e., DAV) Organization, there was no significant difference between the opinions of President George W. Bush and those of Senator John F. Kerry on several key issues recast into questions posed to them by the DAV. These issues included such items as: 1) To make veterans a national priority; 2) to support legislation to authorize the VA to revise it premium schedule for Services Disabled Veterans Insurance (i.e., SDVI) in order to reflect the current mortality tables; 3) to propose or support legislation to increase the face value of SDVI; and, finally, 4) to propose or support legislation to authorize the current receipt of the Survivors Benefit Plan (i.e., SBP) and Dependency and Indemnity Compensation (i.e., DIC) provided by the VA.

When one considers that both candidates expressed these personal opinions before the election, during September and October of 2004, the legislation needed after the national election to initiate the necessary changes has not occurred. Here again, is the wide gulf existing between our Morals (i.e., the "Should Be") and the Mores (i.e., the "I's"); in this case, to resolve the issues noted above.

Quite clearly, the choices made by our political leaders reveal their purity of purpose and truthfulness. Not only do pressure groups thrive in our national capital to influence our leaders, but our elected officials are experts in utilizing the fine art of propaganda. For example, they use the technique of creating issues with programs involving those described above to enact legislation which favors their agenda. Critical issues such as social security and veterans affairs are usually priority items on their agenda. However, how they vote on these issues is a matter of their loyalty to the Republican and Democratic Party, because it is common practice to vote along party lines.

Another technique which is employed is the "band wagon" technique.[19] In this method, the political leader or politician meets informally with his/her colleagues or interested persons to muster support for the particular issue involved. Often, where a close vote looms in the legislature, the politician will cross party lines in order to influence and gain the vote of another politician.

Finally, there are numerous other techniques used by political leaders or others in power which are quite subtle in meaning. For example, Dr. Alfred McClung Lee uses the concept of the "Glittering Generalities—associating something with a 'virtue word'—is used to make us accept and approve the thing without examining the evidence."

For example, virtue words are "good, proper, right, democracy, love," etc. It is a clever technique for the propagandist to focus attention upon a questionable characteristic of the latter "virtue" words because they can mean different things to different people and they can be used in different ways.

However, in my Components of a Culture shown in Figure 1, Sentiments are <u>less</u> generalized and vague and thus they are less prone to be affected. In this case, it is the <u>opinions of a public which the propagandist is intent on changing</u>. Moreover, rather than a criticism of the "virtue words" as we say and understand them, it is a criticism of the uses to which a propagandist puts these words or belief of unsuspecting people.

Consider, for example, the word "democracy." Most Americans would have very definite ideas about democracy because it is the distinctive characteristic of our American Way of Life. From the ideas learned at school, in the home setting, and in churches or synagogues, one would conclude, among other characteristics, that our democracy is a division of power, which division of power is not altered by one without the consent of the other; and that one has the freedom to vote for a favorite candidate for public office.

However, when a political leader or speaker uses the concept as we interpret it, we assume that he/she is employing democracy in a similar manner.

For example, as discussed in Chapter 1, our current war in Iraq was justified for a number of reasons.[21] Among those reasons was that the people of Iraq needed a democratic form of government and self-rule patterned after our form and conception of democracy. This objective for the Iraqi people is a noble one, but our leadership fails to understand the enormous difficulty of this idealistic plan. It defies the practices, conventions, and mores characteristic of our form of democracy and other democracies of the Western world. In actuality, it is glittering generality and a distortion of this vital concept; and it was employed as another excuse for our entry into this war!

Little wonder that there is a feeling of dread which our population feels about our foreign policy in general; and, in particular the great danger we face in the unresolved problems of the Middle East.

In summary, the aforesaid two dominant issues that were used (i.e., social security and the shabby treatment given to our veterans) are prototypes of many others where the art of persuasion has been most effective as a shaping force.

As one strives for meaning and direction in these uncertain and chaotic times, prestige and tolerance are intertwined in our search for a stable identity. These aspects are considered next.

Prestige and Tolerance

Components of a Culture

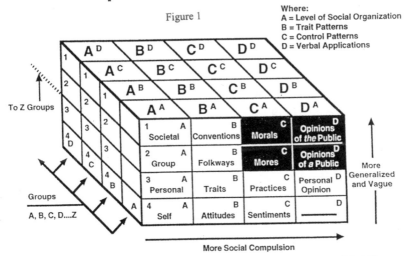

Figure 1

Where:
A = Level of Social Organization
B = Trait Patterns
C = Control Patterns
D = Verbal Applications

To Z Groups

Groups
A, B, C, D....Z

	1 A Societal	B Conventions	C Morals	D Opinions of *the* Public
2	A Group	B Folkways	C Mores	D Opinions of *a* Public
3	A Personal	B Traits	C Practices	D Personal Opinion
4	A Self	B Attitudes	C Sentiments	D ———

More Generalized and Vague

More Social Compulsion

Adapted from <u>The Shaping and Reshaping Forces of Acculturation: A Study of Risk</u>, George Farrah © 1993, St. Coud, MN.

2A Group	2B Folkways
4A Self	4B Attitudes
3C Practices	4C Sentiments

Except for the cultural components of "Group" and "Folkways," definitions have been provided for Traits and Attitudes in previous sections. Since the concepts of Prestige and Tolerance are crucial aspects on one's striving for meaning and identity, as described on pages 72 and 73 of this section, several of the nine values listed affect prestige and tolerance. Also intertwined with the nine values are the three aspects of personality: coping, interacting, and applying.[22]

At first glance, it may be difficult for one to see the relationship or connection between prestige and tolerance and the six cultural components listed beneath them. As used here and throughout my book, "practices" describes all of those characteristics of inner directedness which motivate an individual in his/her actions toward others.[23] As an integral part of a person's private life, the traits, attitudes, sentiments, and practices may not be obvious or evident. Yet, these components play a vital role for the overt or outward expression of one's prestige and tolerance.

Most important, the cultural component of "self," especially in terms of self-concept and motivation, help to define the degree of prestige and outward expression of tolerance and characteristics of personality. As defined, self-concept is how a person views her/his role in terms of a sum total of experiences in life—from work to leisure time activities to interaction with others. The elements of the self-concept include both role expectations (i.e., a positive acceptance of the aspirations and demands that one believes are expected of him/her) and self-adequacy (i.e., the positive regard which one believes are the present and future probabilities of success).[24]

In contrast, the elements of motivation include goal and achievement needs (i.e., how one perceives the intrinsic and extrinsic rewards of one's status and role in life); and personal investment (i.e., the amount of time, energy, and flexibility one is able to exert in order to meet a goal).[25]

The aforesaid elements either propel and enhance feelings of prestige or lower it. In fact, an individual's prestige and security results from the group dynamics of a stable social environment. For example, group members may give prestige and power to those people who possess valued characteristics (i.e., honesty, committed, punctual, etc.) and leadership skills. Conversely, persons of lower prestige or status are more ready to exhibit one type of behavior upward than are persons of higher prestige ready to display the same behavior downward in the social or work environment of the group.[26] In either case of high or low prestige, the cultural components of traits, attitudes, sentiments, and practices are intimately related with the self.

In terms of the "Folkway" described by Summer, as early as 1906, the relations among the groups to which one belongs will profoundly affect one's life. Summer also recognized the significant differences between what he characterized as the functional division of social groups between the "in-group or we-group" and the "out-group" or "others-group."[27]

For example, within the in-group, there is an association of persons toward whom we feel a sense of commonality and mutual identification. These are the people with whom we support the group standard; and with whom we participate by carrying out some group purpose or function. Beginning first with in-group patterns, and, gradually in the acculturation process, the we-group sentiments of familiarity and cohesive solidarity are developed. Conversely, there are also sentiments expressed on oppositional reactions to those groups on the outside.

It is within these in/we group settings that the formative and shaping processes of coping, interacting with others, and applying social skills are learned. The aforesaid sense of commonality is reflected in the expression of ideas, values, and feelings by comments such as, "we act; we feel; we believe, and we belong." The members of this group have a loyalty and obligation to one another. In fact, when a situation arises which is threatening, they will defend one another and express their deepest love and sympathy.

In dramatic contrast, the out-group is an association of persons who experience a lack of tolerance from those in/we groups. The attitudes involve the sentiments of disgust, fear, antagonism, and hatred. Since there is no loyalty, cooperation or sympathy for them, one is prejudiced against members of the others-group. Consider these expressions by the in/we group: "the family down the street is inferior to our own; our neighborhood is better than the one on the other side of the tracks; and one's race is superior to another." Therefore, this lack of tolerance reflects the prejudices and hatred directed toward some out-groups. However, in a time of peace, the attitudes toward out-groups are somewhat milder than in a time of war.[28]

Finally, as a dominant and pervasive feature of social organization, the folkways and polemics of in-group versus out-group comes into play. The concept of ethnocentrism is often applied when those in one group consider themselves as the very center of everything worthwhile. It is a common practice among civilized or savage peoples.

In his brilliant interpretation of folkways in the American Way of Life, Summer was extremely perceptive in his vision that industrial America was undergoing a profound change. In effect, he believed that we were moving from a more personal-homogeneous society to one that was impersonal and heterogeneous. In fact, at the present time, such vital issues as diversity and a greater tolerance for all Americans have been incorporated into the practices of most businesses and organizations. Within our democracy, tolerance of other viewpoints is crucial for its survival.

However, in the acculturation process, particularly in the shaping forces of education, where considerable progress has already been made, both the practice of tolerance and the choices we make should receive more emphases in the content areas that are taught. Since the sentiment, attitudes, and practices of tolerance result from both rational judgment from the mind and from our habits of the heart, it is ironic and tragic that more emphasis is not placed on the teaching of values. Consequently, with the stressing of values in the curriculum, much of the misunderstanding associated with the concept of diversity—not as a divisive process, but as a unifying element—can be eliminated. This latter emphasis will result in a greater understanding of how our heterogeneous country reflects diversity in terms of talent, occupation or position, ability, and interests.

In summary, as one strives for meaning and identity, prestige and tolerance are two vital and inter-related factors. There is a strong relationship between them and the cultural components of group, folkways, self, attitudes, practices, and tolerance. While prestige is essentially how one views oneself, tolerance is that special quality of one not being judgmental of a person or group.

The polarity between spirituality and materialism are also important considerations for the section that follows.

Materialism versus Spirituality

Components of a Culture

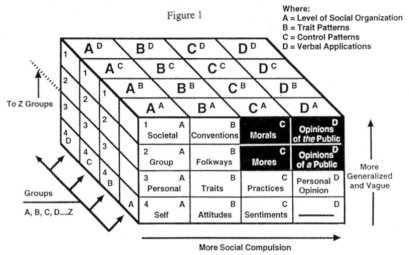

Figure 1

Where:
A = Level of Social Organization
B = Trait Patterns
C = Control Patterns
D = Verbal Applications

Adapted from The Shaping and Reshaping Forces of Acculturation: A Study of Risk, George Farrah © 1993, St. Coud, MN.

1C	3C
Morals	Practices
2C	4C
Mores	Sentiments

In our daily lives, there are many material requirements that are necessary for existing in an era where all sorts of technological innovations have altered our way of life. The practices are affected by the basic needs for shelter, food, drink, societal order, and by the need for protection and security. While these primary needs are characterized by immediacy, there are also secondary needs that are more latent in the mores.

For example, the secondary needs involve artistic, religious, and recreational expression. It is within the domain of latency that spirituality becomes more formalized. From a previous section dealing with "Changes in Orthodoxy" (i.e., see p. 77), since faith is crucial to spirituality, this faith is faith in the invisible. Again as noted earlier, faith in the visible is the immediately apprehended aspect of materialism, and, is therefore, less formalized.

While there is nothing bad or evil in materialism being necessary to our very existence, it is the delicate balance between materialism and spirituality that produces a difference in the values of acculturation such as how one reacts to success, failure, change or something new and different. Conversely, the values we hold can also produce a difference in materialism and spirituality.[29] These values are the directional force in the constant, hourly and daily choices we make in our encounters or interactions with others; be they family members, business associates, significant others or strangers.

In a most practical way, a code of values is really a standard of living—a philosophy of life of what we think and do, rather than merely what we "say."[30] It represents a general plan for the realization of latent ambitions and the eventual attainment of realistic goals. It also reveals our ultimate purpose in life, and, strengthened by the depth of our spirituality—whatever belief that provides us with inner strength and peaceful comfort— our future existence after death.[31] This purity of purpose and truthfulness are motivational factors for those goals that we are willing to live for, and die for—if necessary!

Unfortunately, for so many of our citizens in the American Way of Life, the negative aspects of materialism have cast a spell over them to spend and consume goods and services beyond their actual needs. Via the messages they receive from television commercials and other forms of advertising, people spend and borrow far more than their incomes allow. Then most states legalize and allow gambling by flooding stores with lottery tickets of various kinds for consumers to purchase, despite the tragic fact that so many, with poverty level incomes, are the very ones who buy these tickets! Their desire and hope for winning is so intense that the real odds against winning does not deter them from gambling. Casinos at various geographical locations are also other opportunities for our citizens—regardless of age, gender, occupation, race, income, or educational level—to gamble away their money.

Why has this materialism become so pervasive? Is it because of our false hope, day dreams, or fantasies about becoming instantly rich? Is it because so many have no inspiring philosophy of life? Is it because we are desperate for money?[32] How sad it is that so many in our population live at the poverty level, are homeless and live in a hand-to-mouth dependency, with no particular goal in mind!

There are no easy answers to the complexity of those caught in the vortex of our rampant materialism. However, with an adequate philosophy of life rooted and anchored in spirituality, the individual can develop the ability to adjust and to cope with the disagreeable and horrific experiences that often characterize life.

There are other advantages or benefits to this great reshaping force of spirituality.[33] For example:

- The spiritually motivated person can minimize the tragedies—as painful as they are—that occur in daily living with hope and courage to continue on.

- Regardless of the faith we practice, only religion assures us—without fear of contradiction—that God is not indifferent to human values and unmindful of human needs.

In summary, spiritual self-realization in the law-abiding environment, helps us to become identified with the latent reality of eternity. Having made this identification, we are not afraid of the dark cloud of materialism that constantly hovers over us. With the inner strength and anchor of spirituality, we can cope with the effects of evil. Most important, for the choices we make in our daily lives, if we are not concerned or indifferent to matters of spirituality or latency, then the consequences of our immediate actions or behavior do not matter!

Fortunately, the ethical imperative of the "Golden Rule" practiced by millions of people in our great country and elsewhere in the world, provide the practical means of realizing an important aspect of spirituality. It is the final consideration for this chapter in the constant search for meaning and identity.

The Golden Rule

Components of a Culture

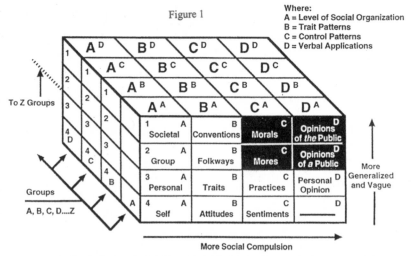

Figure 1

Where:
A = Level of Social Organization
B = Trait Patterns
C = Control Patterns
D = Verbal Applications

Adapted from <u>The Shaping and Reshaping Forces of Acculturation: A Study of Risk</u>, George Farrah © 1993, St. Coud, MN.

3B Traits	3C Practices
4B Attitudes	4C Sentiments

Basic to understanding the dynamics of the interaction process inherent in the golden rule is its value and role in our American ay of Life. Within our form of democracy, one key value and sentiment is the sacredness of the person. Historically, in the Twentieth Century, the latter generalization was evident and stressed in the social-psychological theories of John Dewey, Charles H. Cooley, and George H. Mead.

Quite clearly, in a democracy, the interaction of traits, practices, attitudes, and sentiments—the <u>less generalized</u> components of a culture—involve personal behavior in a number of ways. For example, it allows for situations which are more or less equalitarian give-and-take. In turn, for the persons involved in this interaction, it permits variability of expression, freedom of choice, and voluntary participation in group activities.

Among the many sentiments that guide us in practicing the Golden Rule, the sentiment of love is by far the most powerful shaping force in our behavior toward others.[34] Since the sentiment of love has three characteristics, it helps one to know and understand what they are. The three forms, agape, philos, and eros are all of Greek origin.

First, there is the characteristic of <u>agape love</u>. As an important aspect in religious practice—especially in the Christian faith—it is God's divine love for man. It is also spontaneous and altruistic.

Second, there is the characteristic of <u>eros love</u> or Cupid, the God of love in Greek mythology. This is the romantic love normally expressed between two persons.

Third, there is the characteristic of <u>philos love</u> which is loving or liking another person. It differs from agape and eros in being more inclusive of others. For example, in the historic, wonderful city of Philadelphia, one notes the root word <u>philos</u>. Consequently, from its earliest days, it has been known as the "city of brotherly love."

In terms of practicing the Golden Rule, it is the third characteristic of love, <u>philos</u>, which prevails. It has a dominant theme of kindness when applied to the interaction process between and among individuals.[35] However, for many of us, this simple act of kindness is sometimes difficult to exercise. If we dislike someone for whatever reason, or we harbor a grudge, we can rationalize our behavior for not extending our kindness to this person—especially if he/she is a member of the "out-group" described in a previous section. With our many human weaknesses, this philos love is not always easy to follow.

While it is most difficult to quantify or measure, we know that it varies from person to person, group to group, and from community to community throughout our country. Despite this variance, regardless of location, gender, race, or other characteristics, American people are among the finest in the world! Despite the harsh criticism by others of our country and our people, the traits and practices inherent in the Golden Rule help to guide their behavior in the process of interaction with others.

* *

In summarizing Chapter 2, these generalizations are evident:

- That the Twentieth Century produced new points of entry for the understanding of behavior. The contributions to psychology and psychiatry by the works of Freud, Jung, and others, shed light on the shaping and reshaping forces that converge on the individual. Such concepts as traits, attitudes were given a sharper focus in relation to the components of a culture. Most important, the nine values of acculturation provide a directional force for how one copes, reacts, and applies knowledge in a given situation—especially in terms of "think-how" in addition to "know-how" skills.

- That in terms of religious faith, the dichotomy between vitality and anemia must be bridged if Christianity or other belief systems are to produce a positive difference in the daily lives of our citizens.

- That our political leaders are adept in their use of persuasion and the fine art of propaganda in the decisive legislative bills which they enact. The examples of social security and the needs of Veterans were used as vital issues to be addressed. However, the national leadership has advocated "privatization" in lieu of the present method of funding social security, and adequate funding for the Veterans Administration has not occurred.

- That the formative and shaping processes of coping, interaction with others, and applying social skills greatly affect prestige and tolerance. Prestige can be gained according to one's position, social status, or by possessing valued characteristics or leadership skills. The sentiment and practice of tolerance are dynamically related to the opposing forces of one's belonging to an in-group in contrast to an out-group. However, fortunately, there are people who can transcend this kind of questionable loyalty to any given group, because they believe in the ethical imperatives of decency and respect for others—regardless of race, age, or economic and social status. Therefore, those are the individuals who truly practice the Golden Rule! What choices will you make?

In the dawn of this new century, with the tremendous changes that have occurred with the proliferation and advances in technology, there are serious problems confronting our farmers and the rural way of life. Those challenges are considerations and the substance for Chapter 3.

Endnotes for Chapter 2

[1] Linda Donn, <u>Freud and Jung: Years of Friendship, Years of Loss</u>. See especially Part Four, pp. 135-185. (New York: The Macmillan Co., 1988).

[2] M. Schorer, ed., <u>Criticism: The Foundations of Modern Literacy Judgment</u> (New York: Harcourt, Brace, and World, 1958), p. 118.

[3] G. A. Farrah, <u>A Study of the American Way of Life</u> (Vols. I-III) (St. Cloud, MN: St. Cloud State University, Printing Services, 1977), pp. 7-96.

[4] G. A. Farrah, <u>Handbook on Using the Survey of Academic Values (All Forms)</u> (St. Cloud, MN: St. Cloud State University, Printing Services, 1994), pp. 4-5.

[5] Farrah, Ibid.

[6] G. A. Farrah, Ruth K. Meyer, and Alfred A. Pabst, <u>Leadership and the Transformation of Values</u> (Embry-Riddle Aeronautical University, 1996), pp. 9-10. Presented at Daytona Beach, Florida on November 11, 1996.

[7] Farrah, <u>Handbook</u>, pp. 22-23.

[8] Chris Richards, general ed., <u>World Religions</u> (Rockport, Maine, 1997), pp. 24-178.

[9] Richards, pp. 179-243.

[10] <u>Great Religions of the World</u> (prepared by the National Geographic Book Service), pp. 282-409.

[11] Ibid., pp. 179-243.

[12] Elisabeth Breuilly et al., <u>Religions of the World</u> (New York: Facts on File, 1997), pp. 13, 45, 47.

[13] Dr. Peter B. Clark, consulting ed. <u>The World's Religions: Understanding the Living Faith</u> (Pleasantville, NY: The Reader's Digest Association, 1993), pp. 76-77.

[14] In particular, see the section entitled: Articulate Propaganda and Sensory Reactions: Knowledge by Intuition, pp. 19-24. The more formal, structured sources that shape public opinion result from our mass media and articulate propaganda. In this instance, the quality of leadership plays a significant role.

[15] On the city, state, or national level, a group of individuals may be regarded as "a public."

[16] I was on a funded research project awarded by the Research Committee of St. Cloud State University, St. Cloud, MN, in order to study common core values.

[17] As of this date, April 1, 2005, it is interesting to note the number of articles appearing on the editorial page of newspapers expressing a deep concern in the proposed changes for social security. Typical of these dominant themes of concern, dread, or doubt, are evident in this letter which appeared in the March 31st issue of our Times newspaper in St. Cloud, MN. Consider these themes or opinion which were expressed by this writer: "Bush's social security plan isn't sound---putting money into private accounts would help only the rich---rushing headlong into a risky scheme fueled by fear and rhetoric is not progress (and) --- privatization will leave millions upon millions of workers in this country out in the cold, unable to get by when it comes time for them to enjoy their hard-earned retirement." It is the frequency and consistency of the latter concerns that cast a shadow of doubt on the proposed changes in social security. St. Cloud Times, March 31, 2005, p. 7B.

[18] For example, in its May, 2003 report, the President's Task Force to Improve Health Care Delivery for Our Nation's Veterans identified a significant lack of agreement—really a mismatch—between demands for VA services and the funding available for that purpose. Tragically, the failure to resolve this problem will delay veterans' access to care; it will also affect the quality of care given by dedicated personnel at local centers who are already under considerable pressure. For an excellent analysis of the two candidates' personal opinions or views, see: DAV—The Official Magazine of the Disabled American Veterans

and DAV Auxiliary, Cincinnati, OH, September/October, 2004, pp. 23-27.

[19] While a graduate student at Wayne State University in Detroit, Michigan, it was my good fortune to have taken a sociology course from Dr. Alfred McClung Lee who taught us the fundamentals of propaganda. This superb professor and author of the book entitled, The Fine Art of Propaganda was a great influence on my academic life. Much of the information which I have presented here are ideas I absorbed from his lecture notes and the aforesaid book published in 1972 by Octagon Books, New York, NY. See especially pp. 47-68.

[20] Alfred McClung Lee, Ibid.

[21] In particular, see p. 20 of this book in connection with the ideas developed here.

[22] In one of his books, President Jimmy Carter posed this important question: "What is the origin of these restraints, goals, obligations and promises?" His insightful answer was: "Beginning as infants, we absorb them from our parents, siblings, friends, teachers, from religious experiences and training for our professions, and from government laws, rules for athletic contests, and other accepted norms." These are the building blocks of one's personality in striving for meaning and identity—especially the qualities of prestige and tolerance. From Jimmy Carter, Sources of Strength: Mediations on Scripture for a Living Truth (New York: Random House, 1997), p. 223.

[23] Carter, Ibid. He also stated that "There must be a commitment for us to honor—many types of commitments shape our lives."

[24] G. A. Farrah, Norman J. Milchus, and Willing Reitz, The Self-Concept and Motivation Inventory (SCAMIN: What Face Would You Wear? Manual of Interpretation (Dearborn Heights, MI: Personometrics Co., 1968), pp. 1-9.

[25] Farrah, Milchus, and Reitz, Ibid.

[26] Darwin Cartwright and Alvin Zander, Group Dynamics: Research and Theory (Evanston, IL: Row, Peterson and Co., 1953), pp. 418-419.

[27] For an excellent interpretation of W. S. Summer's origination of the concept of Folkways, published in 1906, see Personality and Problems of Adjustment, by Kimball Young (New York: F. S. Crofts and Co., 1947), pp. 130-131.

[28] Young, Ibid.

[29] William S. Sadler, Practice of Psychiatry (St. Louis: The C. V. Mosby Co., 1953), pp. 537-539.

[30] Sadler, pp. 1004-1016.

[31] Herman A. Preuss, A Theology to Live By (St. Louis: Concordia Publishing House, 1977), pp. 180-182.

[32] M. Scott Peck, M.D., The Road Less Traveled and Beyond (New York: Simon & Schuster, 1997), pp. 224-238.

[33] Peck, pp. 273-278.

[34] M. Scott Peck, pp. 206-215. Here Dr. Peck wisely cautions us that "To do battle with institutional societal evils, we need to remember that what we call good must be good for most people, most of the time, and not merely a matter of 'Is it good for me.' This variant of the Golden Rule means that when we employ double standards condoning our own behavior but judging others harshly for the same breach or something lesser, we are in danger." For example, there are many in our inner cities who receive longer prison terms than others for committing minor crimes.

[35] Rev. John Powell, S. J., Unconditional Love (Allen, TX: Tabor Publishing, 1978), pp. 83-89.

CHAPTER THREE

THE CHALLENGES TO FARMING
AND THE RURAL WAY OF LIFE

The Setting and An Analysis of Four Interviews

Components of a Culture

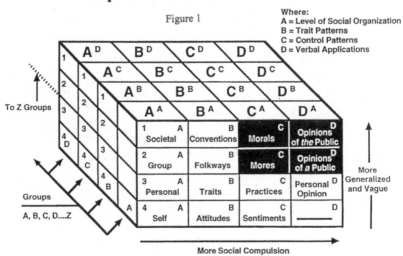

Figure 1

Where:
A = Level of Social Organization
B = Trait Patterns
C = Control Patterns
D = Verbal Applications

Adapted from *The Shaping and Reshaping Forces of Acculturation: A Study of Risk*, George Farrah © 1993, St. Cloud, MN.

As a group of Americans who take pride in being stewards of the land, the practice of farming—particularly the small farm—

3C Practices	2A Group
4C Sentiments	3A Personal

is at-risk in most of our states. Without doubt, these challenges result from a complexity of factors leading to this condition or status of risk.

The motivation for writing this chapter about the looming crisis in farming stems initially from a nationwide and cross-cultural (i.e., Germany, Denmark, and Spain) funded research project conducted by me during the mid-seventies. It involved surveying hundreds of persons via both questionnaires and interviews concerning several categories—of which farming was one—related to our American way of life. Considering the dynamic changes that occurred during the latter half of the twentieth century, the challenges to farming and the rural way of life have been—and continue to be—most dramatic.

Therefore, in obtaining relevant first-hand information for this chapter, I have interviewed several persons—three who are now retired—who are knowledgeable about both the many challenges and risks confronting the farmer. For example, on September 27, 2005, I was invited to Bagley, Minnesota, in order to conduct interviews with my three long-time friends, now retired, concerning the aforesaid challenges. There was Darol Melby, who had been employed by the U.S. Department of Agriculture and the U.S. Soil Conservation Services.

In addition to Darol's useful and productive career with the U.S.D.A. which he began in 1957, he also was employed by the U.S. Soil Conservation Service for 21 years. There he also spent 14 years with the Farmers' Home Administration, and after 35 years of dedicated service in these important endeavors, he finally retired. However, since Darol is acutely aware of the conditions in North Dakota, where wheat farming has been declining in recent years, he continues to offer his able assistance and wisdom to those working with financially stressed farm families.

There was also Albert Toriseva who was at one time, the Superintendent of Schools for the Bagley community; and James Martin, a former teacher and elementary administrator in the Bagley system. Not only was Al an educator; he and his family operated a small farm with a small beef cow-calf herd to supplement his income as an educator. Having grown up on a farm elsewhere in Minnesota, James was also well qualified to share his views.[1]

Then, in addition to the latter interviews in Bagley, it was my good fortune to also interview Bob Lefebvre on October 4, 2005. Bob is the Executive Director of the Minnesota Milk Producers Association, located in nearby Waite Park, Minnesota. These four individuals possess a wealth of knowledge and first-hand experiences about the challenges and issues confronting farmers in general and dairy farmers in particular. Bob was also raised on a farm.[2]

Most important, in considering the components of a culture for this particular section, all interviewees agreed that the components of practices, sentiments, group, and personal—despite considerable overlap—are crucial and necessary if one is to truly understand the challenges to farming. Among the four components, practices becomes a highly personal matter for the farmer and his family. Since family members are also involved in ensuring the success of a particular harvest, a division of labor or responsibilities and planning are necessary.

Following this descriptive setting as a prelude, the dominant themes extracted from those interviewed will be presented, as well as the relevant, basic questions I asked in order to elicit their responses. Therefore, in the following narrative, I am using the rural, farming community of Pierz, Minnesota as a prototype. Having done a school study for the Pierz Public Schools during 1982, I gained a considerable amount of knowledge concerning this rural community.[3] It is really a prototype of so many rural communities in Minnesota where farming is a way of life for so many of its fine citizens.

While it is beyond the scope of this section to provide a complete historical analysis of these rural, farming communities in Minnesota, there are certain characteristics of the Pierz community that are also typical of others across America. While the community of Pierz is approximately 40 miles northeast of the city of St. Cloud, the distinction between a more rural Pierz area and the more urban St. Cloud is less pronounced. Advances in technology via communications and transportation have brought the rural and urban communities closer together, thus making differences less obvious. Yet, there still exists serious differences and points of tension between the rural and urban ways of life as perceived by the farmers.

A dominant characteristic of the Pierz community is the present diversity of its residents. Their ethnic heritage, reflecting a rich historical legacy, can be traced to many parts of the "New World," and to the world in general. For example, as Minnesota developed a diversified economy while still offering unoccupied accessible land in its western parts, a large number of Germans also moved directly there. During 1869, the state agent at Milwaukee observed that 1600 Germans went through that city between May 24 and July 14 enroute to Minnesota. Then, the next year 2,530 arrived via Chicago. During the last peak of German immigration, from 1879 to 1882, with 250,630 arriving in 1881 alone, comparatively fewer settled as farmers in the German pioneer region of the Minnesota Valley. Instead, more went to the cities of St. Paul, Minneapolis, and Duluth.

Gradually, with the influx of immigrants from all parts of Europe, Pierz revealed another dominant characteristic: its deep spirituality. This spirituality was reflected in all aspects of community life from its view of the cohesive family; its churches; its perspective of education; its inspiring patriotism;

its capacity for hard work; and its reverence for tradition. Yet, so typical of diverse populations, there were often problems that made reaching a consensus or agreement, especially in terms of social issues, very difficult. However, the basic question to these farmers then and now is: how can my efforts be profitable in order to survive in my rural community?[4]

By the end of the nineteenth century, similar to Pierz, the rural areas of America had made the science of agricultural an imperative, a characteristic way of life from birth to death. Thanks to these early settlers, in the prairie land of the Midwest and elsewhere in our country, the forest was cleared, and homes were gradually replacing the earlier cabins. Except for some swampy sections, whenever the soil was fertile and not marginal, farming was an ideal way of life.

Therefore, taking advantage of nature's gifts of excellent soil conditions, an adequate water supply, and a favorable, rhythmic climate, these farmers gave their attention to the art and science of agriculture. Consequently, they carefully cultivated hundreds of acres of corn, rye, oats, and wheat—sometimes for animal husbandry and sometimes not.

During these formative years, agriculture communities seemed to escape the hustle and bustle so characteristic of city life and the urban dweller. Yet, in this rural setting, a number of enterprises or occupations emerged as a result of persistent cultivation of crops or producing milk via the dairy farm. As in most agricultural communities in America, especially in a non-mechanized age, one can imagine the presence of blacksmiths, tanneries, shoemakers, coopers, carpenters, potash workers, and general stores that serviced this agrarian way of life.

Very slowly, almost imperceptibly, there were considerable and dynamic changes within twentieth century America. For better or worse, those changes had a profound impact on the farmer's way of life. For example, the farmer was thrown into a maelstrom of a fluctuating economy over which he had little or no control; and he gradually became dependent on expensive machinery and fertilizers, which increased his efficiency or crop yield, but left him at the mercy of an impersonal pricing system—especially with the speculative practices of a "futures market." He also acquired an awareness (despite efforts to control his land use) of a distant bureaucracy in Washington, D.C. whose politically motivated farm policies were often at odds with his immediate situation, his problems, or his needs. Nevertheless, in this quiet rural setting, there was a note of comfort, a pride and passion for hard work, and a strong religious faith; in brief, the cherishment of rural values. Thus, while the present setting of life on the rural farm has changed dramatically, one would not be too surprised to observe that the ethical imperatives of rural living still remain.

Let us now turn to the results of the interviews which I conducted at Bagley on September 27, 2005 and the results of the interview I did at Waite Park on October 4, 2005, which follows.

Results From the Interview at Bagley, Minnesota

For each of the questions asked, the responses provided by each of the three who participated will be indicated by their name which appears in parentheses before their response (i.e., Darol, Al, or James. The same procedure is used for the interview which follows this one).

My first question asked:

"What do you think the challenges are to farming in Minnesota?"

- (Darol) Here, in Clearwater County, we are not in the mainstream of agricultural production. We have crop land, pasture land and forest land. We have many avenues from which we collect an income. If we look at the past, we look at forestry as a major enterprise. Thus, with the clearing of the land, little fields became larger fields. But in today's agriculture, I still use the term of "patch farming." We do not have the landscape that lends itself to large farming operations.[5] So, after World War II, we had an influx of returning G.I.s who wanted to be farmers like their parents. Then there was a transition to depopulation from the 1950's to the 1980's, because people could no longer make a living on the farm. Therefore, these small farms that once supported a family, could no longer do so. So people on the farms went to where the jobs were. Yet, there was a return of certain kinds of non-farm jobs, either to the regional center at Bemidji or here in Bagley. But the primary non-farm jobs now are manufacturing with one local company accounting for 300 jobs. We also have the county court house system and the nursing home with another 300 jobs; then we have the school system which employs 150 persons. Nevertheless, our citizens go to Bemidji or surrounding areas in order to work or find employment. This agricultural area as such, is no longer a concern of depopulation, but can be described as a stabilized population. From 1960 to now, our population averaged about 8,500. Therefore, I do not foresee agriculture as becoming a major factor because we live in an area where we farm a little bit; but one member of the family has to work off the farm to sustain family living.

  Thus, if we are to look into the future for twenty or thirty years, I do not see an increase in agriculture production.

- (Myself) Darol, from the perceptive remarks and analyses which you just gave, there has been and continues to be a serious economic challenge confronting the farmer. Your remarks prompt this question: "Is this economic challenge unique to Clearwater County and other rural areas of Minnesota or is it occurring elsewhere in our country?"

- (Darol) George, yes, the economic challenge is also occurring in the states west of us. In fact, because the federal subsidies favor the mega or large farms—those farms averaging 1,000 to 5,000 acres—depopulation of the small farms in rural areas will take place. Since a great deal of capitol is required in order to sustain that type of agriculture, the younger generation of people who farm will never be able to get into those much larger operations.[6] For example, those commercial farms receive payments of hundreds of thousands of dollars from our federal government in comparison to the small farm which receives just hundreds of dollars from the same source.

- (Myself) Your analyses will be most helpful, Darol. What have been your experiences, Al?

- (Al) For many years, I discovered that the raising of beef cattle on our small farm helped to supplement my income as an educator. With long hours of hard work and the help of my family, it was a reasonably successful operation—in spite of market prices which varied from season to season. With some periods of low prices for beef cattle, I barely broke even.

- (Myself) Quite clearly, Al, you diversified your time, energy and talents to make your raising of beef cattle a success over the years. However, with your children, now adults and away from you, and, being retired, this operation is no longer in existence. Another important question I have for you relates to how you believe technology has affected farming—would you share your thoughts or experiences on this item?

- (Al) The availability and use of energy or fuel is a critical concern for Americans in general and the farmer in particular.

The cost of fuel is causing the demise of the family farm. The neighboring dairy farm, operated by a father and son (milking 70 cows) in August 2005 refueled their three farm tractors for a total cost of $700.00. They fueled their two ground fuel storage tanks to the amount of $3,800.00 while the price they get paid for milk has continued to decline over the present year. The family farm will not be able to survive.[7]

For example, in terms of better mileage for the vehicles we drive, there have been valid reports and verifiable evidence of inventions that can vastly improve their performance. Yet, I suspect that any invention or innovation that promises to decrease our fuel consumption never makes it to the market place.

- (Myself) How about the use of computers; are farmers becoming adept or skillful in their use?

- (Al) To the best of my knowledge, those who do are able to collect all kinds of data relating to storing information. For example, they can make a comparative analysis of the yield of any given crop from year to year. Therefore, the computer provides a reliable database for cost analysis or planning for the future—especially in view of fluctuating prices in a futures market. However, for those farmers who are not knowledgeable about how to use a computer but would like to learn, often the pressure and long hours of work on the farm preclude the opportunity for him to take classes or receive formal training.[8]

- (Myself) Those are very insightful comments Al, relating to challenges and many thanks for sharing your ideas. Yet I know that there are shaping forces that have an impact on the farmer's practices, and one force involves values. Jim, from your experiences and knowledge of one who grew up on a farm in a rural area, would you now share with us how values influence the farmer, or the relationship between values and agriculture?

- (Jim) Yes, of course. I have summarized my thoughts in the following manner:

Most important from my perspective, Dr. William Glasser states in his book, Reality Thinking, that we all have the psychological need to love and to be loved. In other words, he says that we all must learn "social responsibility" or the skills to "care for" each other and to be cared for. By growing up in a rural/agricultural setting, we had many opportunities to learn this caring. For example, if someone in the community was ill or injured, everyone (including children) was expected to pitch in and help saw wood; gather or harvest crops; and take care of farm animals.

We also had extended families, 4-H Clubs, church groups, and local schools in which to learn "social responsibility." From an early age on, we walked in the shadow of uncles, aunts, and grandparents.

- (Myself) What wonderful models to follow! What did you learn from them, Jim, and how has this acculturation process changed?

- (Jim) We learned their values and practices of honesty, kindness, and hard work. Computers and television have now become the "value translators" and shaping forces for so many of our vulnerable children![9]

Chores on the farm taught us much! We were given jobs and it was expected that we would do our share. These various tasks on our farm gave us the feeling that we were

<u>needed</u> and were contributing to the good of all. These chores also taught us that hard work pays off; and, most important, that we were valuable contributors.[10] As our models, our parents were part of a generation that valued both hard work and education. Accordingly, they wanted their children to have it better than they did; and, therefore, they realized that education and hard work were necessary for achieving results for the present and the future.[11]

Farms were diversified in the past—so children growing up like me became generalists. For example, we knew about crops, cows, pigs, chickens, gardening, etc. Since then, and in contrast, farms have become so specialized now that the farmer's knowledge may be deeper, but not as broad as in the past. In effect, now, they have put all of their eggs in one basket!

- (Myself) Thanks, Jim, for giving us your valuable comments about the close relationship between values and agriculture.

* *

After returning to St. Cloud following my group interview with Darol Melby, Al Toriseva, and Jim Martin at Bagley, I arranged for my final interview with Bob Lefebvre on October 4, 2005. In the transcript of the interview which follows, this Executive Director of the Minnesota Milk Producers Association also provided extremely vital information relating to the challenges of farming.

Results From an Interview at Waite Park, Minnesota

- (Myself) Bob, I deeply appreciate your willingness to grant me this interview regarding what you perceive to be the challenges to dairy farmers in general and to other farmers in particular. To begin, would you share your views regarding these challenges?

- (Bob) The challenges for the dairy producers come down to two fundamental things: the dairy farmer must make enough money to be profitable and to have a good quality of life.[12] Those are very basic needs to any of our citizens.

- (Myself) You are referring to the American Way of Life?

- (Bob) Yes; these are the two fundamental challenges: first, to make more money in order to be profitable; and second, to improve the dairy farmers' way of life. Therefore, the challenges they face have to deal with those things. Now, how can they do that? Dairy farmers have the trait of being independent. For example, what one dairy farmer thinks is the best for being profitable in his situation varies considerably with what another dairy farmer thinks. We see models in the western United States and the southwestern United States and many other places where there are very large dairy operations.

- (Myself) Bob, would you classify these large operations as "Mega Farms?"

- (Bob) Yes; and we have some of them in Minnesota, too, of 5,000 or more cows. But that's okay too, if that is what the farmer thinks is best for him. That's one model if he wishes to go that way.

Another model is where the farmer needs fewer capitol resources and less building structure. Again, whatever the model, the challenge is for us to help the farmer meet his goal. In Minnesota, an environment should be created— both on the state and local level—that encourages a process of independence. For example, if the farmer wants to expand, he should be allowed to do so. If he wants to expand his operation, let him do that.

- (Myself) So there is diversity among dairy farmers in terms of purpose, time, space, and flexibility.

- (Bob) Absolutely! It's quite different than other types of lifestyles. Yet, we have had divisiveness among our dairy farmers. Some producers will say: "You should be doing it my way. You should only be milking forty cows. If you milk any more than forty cows, you're a bad person." Now we've seen a lot less of that. For example, dairy farmers are beginning to appreciate other dairy producers doing it the way they want to do it. I've been trying to create a balance between those two positions or viewpoints, and we're making some progress. The bottom line is that these challenges come down to a number of things. In order for the farmer to have a net income equal to what the average Minnesotan's income is, you have to have a certain number of cows. You can also supplement that income from milking cows.

- (Myself) Can you give me an example of your last comment, Bob?

- (Bob) Yes, of course. Michelle, who works with our organization and is a member of our team, lives on a farm. Her husband and father-in-law operate a dairy farm in addition to their other jobs.

- (Myself) Are these situations or challenges unique to Minnesota or are there similarities elsewhere?

- (Bob) I think that you will find that, where dairy farming has a long-standing set of traditions of living a part of that industry for a long period of time, you will find some similarities between Minnesota and Wisconsin; and between Minnesota and Pennsylvania.

- (Myself) How about Michigan?

- (Bob) Less so in Michigan maybe.

- (Myself) Why is that so?

- (Bob) Because it's related to those states which have a long tradition of dairy farming. There is, like Minnesota, a long history of dairy farming; which has been there for generations, a strong dairy or large dairy infrastructure if you will. There have been other sections of the country where there has always been dairy farming there, but they don't have quite the tradition. They have expanded much quicker than we have because I think that they had to. The bottom line is: we would have seen more dairy producers expanding—if they had to or if they thought it was necessary. In effect, those who expanded sooner did it out of necessity.

There are other states much further along than we are. Minnesota has had a history of losing farms and losing milk producing activities.[13] We've had a wide spectrum of producers who have been able to make money and we've had others who were not as successful.

- (Myself) In view of our losing farms—especially within the last decade—what has happened to the rural way of life?

- (Bob) I would say that there are actually a couple of components to the rural way of life.

First of all, what makes up rural America? A large part of it is the dairy farmer. Now, obviously, the rural environment, the atmosphere, is also cherished by the city dweller.

Second, and it becomes a point of tension for the dairy farmer, the person from the city feels a need to move out. By this move, they, too, can enjoy the rural way of life. There is a little bit of a complication there: the rural way of life is hampered by this. Consider the work schedule of the dairy farmer. For example, there are long working hours, even day and night at certain times of the year which affect his life style. The former urban dweller tries to change that with the city oriented value system and it has a negative effect for the dairy farmer.

- (Myself) Bob, how does the city oriented value system differ from the rural one?

- (Bob) It is less personal and more hurried. In effect, those who move out of urban centers or cities have jobs there. That's not the rural way of life! The rural way of life is the land—an asset radically different than having land for the purpose of building a home for residential purposes.

- (Myself) Then the dairy farmer, like other farmers of crops and cattle, are really stewards of the land. Would that generalization fit your idea of the rural way of life?

- (Bob) Yes. The farmer cares for that land while he is alive. He grows the crops, feeds the animals, milks the cows, tills the soil, plants the seeds, fertilizes the soil, weeds the crops, and does other tasks in order to bring in a successful harvest. From these practices, they are able to maintain their viability and livelihood off of this asset of land.

We have some towns like Melrose, for example. It's a dairy-based community; yet, we have some urbanites moving out trying to change that.

- (Myself) That is an interesting point, Bob. In what way do you think these former city residents—you refer to them as urbanites—are trying to change the rural practices of the dairy farmer?

- (Bob) While the newcomers to these former farm lands have moved to their new homes in order to enjoy the countryside as a "bedroom community" of an urban area, the farmer exerts all of his energy and time to make his land productive. From the milk of his cows, he creates butter, cheese, or other dairy products. Those products help him and his family to survive.[14]

On the other hand, you can go to other parts of Minnesota, southwestern Minnesota, for example, where you see the town dieing. What's amazing is, from that productive land, they are exporting their crops of soybeans out of that area. They are not using their land or putting value into it by raising cows; turning milk into butter; and doing other practices of the dairy farmer. In effect, urbanites take that land base, build a house on it, create more burden for the community's governmental services, and continue their practice of commuting to town.

- (Myself) What other impact do the urbanites have on the rural way of life?

- (Bob) They simply take away the rural habits—they really do. Take the town of Litchfield: They have urbanites who commute from Edina in the Twin Cities area from their employment there to their homes built in Litchfield. Therefore, they are not adding anything to dairy farming; rather, they are taking away. I believe that presently, there is friction between the urban and rural way of life.[15] If you're taking land as a developer, you should be truly developing that land to be productive.

On the other hand, if the dairy farmer receives a lucrative offer for his land from a land developer, and he sees the potential of making money more than he could by farming, he will be tempted to sell.

- (Myself) Bob, considering the various challenges which you have described, what is your highest priority?

- (Bob) My job is to keep dairy producers milking cows. I would rather see them re-invest in their dairy operation as a viable business rather than someone else come in and alter it or continue the operation without improving it. It might sound harsh but the urbanite should not be encouraged by developers who are out for the big buck to encroach on the land or life of the struggling farmer.

Most important, a critical objective in farming and the rural life it embraces is about feeding a nation and feeding a world. A dairy farm doesn't put enough strain on governmental services and farmers pay their fair share of taxes. We cannot allow a vocal minority within various levels of government to make or control policies that affect the dairy farmer.

George, there is another component that you mentioned that is very interesting. You spoke of "Cultural aspects" in relation to the farmer. There is also another group that likes to attach themselves to agriculture. I would say that this group is characterized by having a higher income. More often than not, their values and personal agendas are not congruent with those of farmers in terms of objectives and goals.

- (Myself) Would you comment on the social concept or cultural vitality and the affirmation of the rural way of life that farmers in general embrace?

- (Bob) Farmers still have the same values. They have held to those values in our American way of doing things with the traits of honesty and a purity of purpose. Consequently, they have held to those values longer than most other Americans. The farmer today—whether they are organic producers or whether they are milking five thousand cows or five cows—have the same values. They are very strong family oriented "individuals", they believe strongly in "the family structure"; they believe in doing business locally because they understand the need for a personal relationship as well as a business relationship; they care for their cows and their animals; and, most important, they work in order to enjoy their free time.

- (Myself) Those are very vital and interesting topics that you discussed, Bob. Let's move on now to another topic. What role or impact do you think technology has had on the farmer?

- (Bob) There's a new development in technology that was just announced a couple of weeks ago. There is no question that technology has altered many practices of the farmer, especially egg production practices. Most of the technology being researched, developed, focused, and introduced in agriculture is aimed at doing more with less. This technology helps to add to the size, the scope the farmer needs to have in order to be successful. It means that, in order to keep up with the competitive atmosphere brought on by these developments, I have to get a little bit bigger. I mentioned this to the representative who came out from this company with this latest piece of technology. I commented that it has the potential of having a relatively large impact for dairy production. It would be nice if we used technology to help increase the demand on our products. For example, by improving the quality of our product, we could produce milk that could cure cancer or do a number of things; and thus it would increase the demand for our products. Every time we have the introduction of a new technology it causes a shift in supply and demand and we go through a larger deficit in the industry. It results in fewer farms, and, then, in time, larger farms. The rural way of life thus experiences a new dimension.

- (Myself) In other words, there can be more creative ways of using milk.

- (Bob) Absolutely! Years ago, we would milk the cows and use the cream; make cheese and butter out of it; and the "whey" would be a waste product. With the new technology we have been able to understand that. Now we have been able to extract more of the nutrients—such as whey—and other good components from milk. As a result of these innovations, we have been able to sell more product. In fact, in Minnesota we have a company that leads in the production of whey protein products.

- (Myself) How many dairy producers do we have in our state?

- (Bob) There are about 2000 of them in Minnesota.

- (Myself) In terms of your organization, how often do you meet?

- (Bob) We meet twice a year and then have one big meeting once a year in St. Cloud. We have had them outside of St. Cloud a couple of times, but, mainly, they are held in St. Cloud each year—for thirty years now. We have, in addition to myself, leadership which is supplied by our Board of Directors who provide us with a sense of direction. Our leadership supplies our farmers with knowledge and educational information to help them succeed.

- (Myself) At the present time, what is the major concern of the dairy farmers in your organization?

- (Bob) Their major concern and worry is about urban sprawl. It is a huge issue for them. It is all about land use as I touched on earlier; namely, how to make a living from farming when people continue to move out of cities and encroach on land for farming.

- (Myself) Bob, your comments have been so helpful in discussing the challenges and issues which are vital to the dairy farmer in particular and farming in general, here in Minnesota and elsewhere. I thank you for taking the time and effort to share your expertise and knowledge with me.

* * * * * * * * * * * * * * * * * *

In addition to the endnotes which I have used to embellish or buttress the wealth of information gained from the above interviews, these generalizations are appropriate to summarize the challenges to farming and its way of life.

1. That dynamic changes within twentieth century America have had a profound impact on the farmer's way of life by the shaping forces of economics, politics, and social events.

2. That small farms, which once supported a family, and, indirectly, a community's very existence, can no longer do so.

3. That those communities no longer in the mainstream of agricultural production depend on other avenues for their income.

4. That since one member of the family has to work off the farm in a nearby city to sustain family living, agriculture, alone, is not a major factor. Therefore, in the years ahead, an increase in agricultural production is unlikely.

5. That because subsidies from the federal government favor or are partial to the mega or large farms, depopulation of the smaller farms in rural areas will take place in the future.

6. That since a great deal of capital is required to sustain a mega farm, the younger generation who farm will have considerable difficulty in getting into those much larger operations.

7. That technology has produced innovation and efficient equipment for farming, but the rising price of fuel to operate this equipment is a critical concern for American farmers. The availability and quality of water is another major concern.

8. That by growing up in a rural agricultural setting, young people had many opportunities to practice values unique to life on a farm. With the demise of the small farm, those opportunities will diminish.

9. That in order to succeed, the dairy farmer must make enough money to be profitable; succeed in his mission; and to improve his way of life.

10. Dairy farmers have the trait and practice of being independent in determining the most profitable methods to succeed. There are several models throughout our country ranging from small dairy farms to the large or mega operations. It is important for the industry to achieve a balance among these models.

11. With the increase of urban sprawl and the values of the city dweller brought to the rural area in terms of a new residence, it has a negative impact for the dairy farmer. Whereas the rural way of life centers on the land, it is radically different than having a few acres for a residential home and then commuting on a daily basis to a job in the city.

Finally, the challenges to farming and the rural way of life described in this chapter has put the small farms and rural way of living at risk. The ramifications for the future of our country in terms of our food supply are serious and must be addressed by the decision-makers at all levels of government, both nationally and locally.

In Chapter 4, an examination is made relating to the Western style of democratic processes and divisions of power.

Endnotes for Chapter 3

[1] These three individuals that were interviewed are long-time residents of the Bagley community and are highly respected for their contributions in education and agriculture.

[2] As the Executive Director of his organization, Bob Lefebvre brings a wealth of farming experience to his leadership role.

[3] From a research project conducted by the author entitled: <u>Elementary School Study; Schools in Harding, Pierz, Lastrup, and Buckman</u>. Published by the Printing Services of St. Cloud State University, May 31, 1982, pp. 1-4. This research project, lasting approximately six years, was made possible by the cooperative efforts and diverse talents of individuals in the Pierz area and adjoining communities as well as individuals at St. Cloud State University and elsewhere. This 149 page publication provided the decision makers in Pierz several alternatives to construct (which they eventually did) an elementary school to serve their district.

[4] Later in this section, the reader will note that this generalization of farming being profitable in order to survive is validated by the interviews conducted in late September and early October, 2005.

[5] Without doubt, the soil in Clearwater County is, at best, marginal in terms of raising profitable crops for the marketplace. However, as one moves westward (i.e., from Bagley) to the Crookston area, the beginning or edge of the Red River Valley, one finds the soil to be ideal for sugar beets, sunflowers, and other crops.

[6] This economics challenge to farming provided by Darol was given impetus by the recently approved "Central American Free Trade Agreement" made by our government with six Latin American countries. The details and ramifications of this agreement will have most serious and unfortunate consequences for agriculture in the United States, especially the farmers in Minnesota whose family farms will be at great risk. For example, exporting countries will be allowed to convert their excess sugar into ethanol, seriously impacting the

economies of the ethanol industry which holds such high promise in Minnesota. For an excellent analysis of the challenge posed by the CAFTA, see the article by Marti Oakley entitled "CAFTA Cuts Agricultural Jobs in State" published by the St. Cloud Times, issue of October 6, 2005 (see the editorial page of Section B, "Local News").

[7] At this writing, the Midwest and our country in general are struggling with the souring cost of fuel. Since farmers rely on diesel fuel, they have been hurt economically by the sharp rise in price for this fuel. For example, those farmers with very large acres of crops could use hundreds of gallons of diesel fuel in order to run their combines, tractors, semi-trucks, or other equipment. Unfortunately, these yearly expenses for fuel have the potential of putting some worthy farmers out of business. For an excellent analysis of this serious problem, see the article by Nick Hanson entitled "Midwest Struggles with Soaring Costs," which appeared in the St. Cloud Times issue of November 2, 2005, p. 3A. Moreover, in an earlier Associated Press release which also appeared in the aforesaid newspaper on May 28, 2005, those farmers in Fresno, California who grow our nation's fruits and vegetables have found planting difficult for them. They say that the rising cost of oil is making this one of their toughest planting seasons yet. In this same article, Terry Francl, senior economics with the American Farm Bureau Federation based in Washington, D.C., had a gloomy forecast. He stated that, "Farmers across the country will spend about 10 percent more this year, or about $3 billion on costs including fuel and the concurrent higher cost for fertilizer." Quite clearly, from the same A.P. release, one learns that California has led the nation in agricultural production since World War II. Imagine, the state's vast Central Valley, more than twice the size of Massachusetts, grows most of the world's almonds, and most U.S. grown nectarines, walnuts, raisins, and many other crops vital to our nation. The demise of farms there would be tragic!

[8] The data and information that the computer-trained farmer can extract from a relevant website can be valuable to him in his daily operations.

[9] Unfortunately, as valuable as computers have become in our way of life, "these value translators" cannot replace the knowledge and wisdom derived from the processes of coping, interacting and applying what we learn directly in our daily encounters with others. In the hierarchy of values, the data and information extracted from computers are both necessary and immediate. However, knowledge and wisdom, gained from careful study and from interaction with others, is more latent and ranks higher than data and information.

[10] These are the qualities and practices that contribute to the healthy formation of character, and the enhancement of self-concept and motivation.

[11] Ibid.

[12] With rising fuel costs and falling milk prices, the dairy farmers in Minnesota learned that during October, 2005, a Congressional Senate agriculture committee voted to revive a federal dairy subsidy. The Milk Income Loss Contract which expired on October 1, 2005, was revived by a Senate vote and this subsidy amounts to $998 million, or a 25 percent cut. This proposed legislation awaits approval by both the Senate and the House. Supporters of the subsidy say many small farms with 125 cows or fewer would go out of business without the aid. Before its expiration the aforesaid subsidy provided more than $163 million to Minnesota farmers and $2 billion to struggling farmers nationwide in the past three years. See the St. Cloud Times issue of October 20, 2005, p. 1A and also the issue of November 10, 2005, p. 1A for the source of these developments.

[13] In terms of dairy farms in other states, there are clashing regional differences in their support of a dairy subsidy. For example, the state of Idaho, where dairy farms are much larger than those in the Northeast and Midwest, via their senatorial representation, wanted to strip the dairy subsidy from a proposed congressional bill. In contrast, states such as Vermont, Pennsylvania, New York, and Wisconsin were in favor of it. The St. Cloud Times, October 20, 2005, pages 1A and 5A.

[14] Quite clearly, the advent of "urban sprawl" and how one uses and controls a plot of land, can generate or create points of tension between the former urban, city dweller and the nearby farmer.

[15] As stated above, here are examples of the points of tension that could exist.

CHAPTER FOUR

DIVISIONS OF POWER: THE WEST RETAINS ITS BELIEF IN DEMOCRATIC PROCESSES

People Should Run the Government: Fact or Fancy?

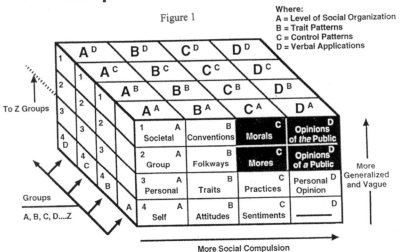

Components of a Culture

Figure 1

Where:
A = Level of Social Organization
B = Trait Patterns
C = Control Patterns
D = Verbal Applications

Adapted from The Shaping and Reshaping Forces of Acculturation: A Study of Risk, George Farrah © 1993, St. Coud, MN.

Since government is the heart and soul of the American Way of Life, where the interaction of all cultural components are involved,

131

1C Morals
2C Mores
3C Practices
4C Sentiments

the components portrayed in Column C above deserve special consideration.

Of all ideas associated with the Western form of government, three seem to, where democracies prevail, persist. These are, first, that people should run their government; second, that their government should not be too strong, and third, that taxation should be based on the person's ability to pay. Historically, over the centuries, there have been more or less conservative to liberal forms of governments; from the divine rights of kings, to parliaments, and from outright dictatorships to democracies.

Yet, despite the aforesaid pressures and the more conservative forces in Western society, people retain the sentiment that they should run their governments via their elected officials. However, one finds that there is considerable political distance between the latter ideal and the actual operation of a government–complete with all bureaucratic support systems.

The problem really involves the discrepancy between the moral–in this case, that "people should run their government"– and the mores, which shows a considerable variance with the moral.

For example, the ideal of a division of power, <u>which division of power is not altered by one party without the consent of another</u>, is an idea that has roots in John Locke. Other political thinkers since then have demonstrated that this idea of government permeates all <u>theoretical</u> aspects of Western life.

Most important, this idea of shared power finds expression in arrangements of all types. It is crucial to unions and management when they "bargain" for items that go into a new contract. It is reflected in the various levels of state, city, county and township governments. It is the cornerstone of the delicate balance that exists among the three branches of government: the executive, the legislative and the judicial.

It is little wonder, then, that this sentiment of self government is so strong in the West. Understandably, since practices differ from country to country, there are variations in style, form, and expression. In parliaments, within the political form of a limited monarchy, the power is shared among two houses and a prime minister. In this latter instance, political accountability may be more expedient and apparent than in the U.S. form.

Consider that in the event of a scandal, or, if for any reason there is a lack of confidence in the government, the opposing party can call for a new election. In contrast to this political safety valve, to date, in the U.S., there has been only <u>one</u> presidential resignation because of a scandal!

Is it because the most recent version of Western democracy does not mind washing its political linen in public? Is it because the political process of electing officials has become intimately associated with one's ability to muster the financial means to support the great expenses of an election? Is it because the tremendous influence of pressure groups, in the form of a permanent, fixed lobby, can dictate the course or outcome of any given election, often in favor of a particular minority at the expense of a majority? These questions, all reflecting unique characteristics of the American political system, are deserving of comment.

First, it is painfully true that Americans, mostly by the media, do not hesitate to chastise or call to an accounting any wrong doing evidenced by a political leader. Regardless of level, be it local, state or national, the individual is scrutinized with a precise, moral microscope! While our citizens are justified and should be commended for their negative assessments of their political leadership whenever it occurs, it remains an ironic practice and sentiment. In fact, the private citizen may also have questionable moral traits; but this same citizen expects his/her leader to be above reproach, free from sin and any kind of wrong doing. Quite clearly, because of various modes of behavior in their private lives, candidates have been forced to drop out of contention for a particular office or governmental seat. Once under the process of media scrutiny, the charges or innuendoes become so intense that the once confident candidate is no longer seriously considered.

In passing, one may examine this longing or yearning for an ideal of political perfection. It is an ethical imperative in a cynical age that looks at politics and politicians as being synonymous with graft and corruption, especially on the national level. Apparently, Americans are comfortable with a system that permits a close inspection of a public official's private life as well as his/her public life. Scandals are really not a unique phenomenon in the West. The paramount difference is how a given government handles it. The "openness" or "silence" about the matter in question is really a matter of degree. While the United States may go the route of impeachment of its highest officials, in Germany or most European countries, in the face of public stigma, the official simply resigns.

Second, the political process of electing officials is closely associated with one's financial resources, which, in turn, sheds light on a potential candidate's power and prestige. In this age of the inflated dollar, it appears that the higher the office to which one ascribes, the more resources it takes to become a serious contender. Even in the case of the presidential candidate, where the government contributes to the candidate's political expenses, the amount allocated does not cover the expenses incurred, and the candidate ends up in debt.

Money, then, or the ability to secure financial backing, has become a crucial ingredient for success. No matter that the candidate is mediocre; that he or she lacks the political vision of a true leader; and that this person conforms to the wishes of influential groups; money, indeed, talks and it is necessary for winning any given election.

One senses that people caught in this Zeitgeist, this winter time of political activity, desperately need leaders of a higher plane. The innocent millions, who retain belief in their cherished democracy, deserve more than the cynical opportunists who use their offices for personal gain. The discerning ear is quick to pick up key phrases used by those on the lower political plane. For example, their speeches are laden with verbal expressions such as "<u>This</u> country" - rather than "Our country" - or "I really want to be honest with you!" In the former phrase, the use of an impersonal pronoun in describing their political allegiance tells something of their true view of their land. After all, an impersonal "<u>this</u> country" makes it much easier to regard government as an <u>object</u>, something to be used or manipulated rather than served! In similar manner, the voters, always hoping for the best from their candidates, also may be used as "objects" for cunning, political manipulation. A campaign promise and an actual voting record may reveal a great discrepancy for many elected officials. Here, again, is the gap between the morals (i.e., the "should be") and the mores (i.e., the actual practices).

Finally, the majority of Americans suffer from the effects of influential pressure groups who maintain effective active lobbies at the national level. Amply funded and with strong organizational designs, these lobbies maintain a close network, distributing information to sympathetic individuals and groups who, in turn, provide volunteer work to achieve a particular goal. At a time when America has been weakened economically and politically, especially in its many commitments to other governments or causes, it does not need a further drain of its youth and resources. Unfortunately, the theoretical checks and balances inherent in the democratic division of power are often missing in realistic practice. One asks: how can any given small country, with long range objectives detrimental to the good of America, wield such enormous power? The lobby sees to that!

With care and precision, the necessary congressional votes are "lined up," so to speak, to ensure the passage or defeat of a particular legislative effort.

While none of the aforesaid description comes as any surprise to the most elementary student of government, one is simply amazed at the existing silent covenants, the conforming opinions, and the closed minds of the powerful decision makers! How can it be that a country so generous, so compassionate and understanding for the "underdog," the poor, the oppressed, maintains a double standard in its desire to be neutral? In fact, by invoking this double standard, it is not neutral!

It is little wonder that the average voter becomes cynical about those entrusted to represent her/his views. One notes a growing distrust, a political disease associated with secrecy and disdain for the wishes of the majority.

With the onset of the years 2006, a new cult of secrecy in our leadership has emerged resulting from our continued involvement in Iraq and elsewhere. No matter how noble or justified the cause, the process of decision-making was distorted to achieve the wishes of the executive branch. No matter that Congress retains important constitutional authority in matters of foreign policies: covert actions became the modus operanti. No matter that serious errors in decision-making may have been committed in the name of misguided loyalty: that delicate balance inherent in a division of power was being upset by the seeds of distrust.

In summary, it is quite clear that indirectly, people do run the government; that via their voting privilege, they have the power to elect or recall office holders; and the power to initiate constitutional changes. These latter are hard facts that are typical in the Western form of government. However, what is not clear is whether the elected officials truly represent those voters who trusted their leaders to carry out a given promise or mandate. If one argues that it is "idealism" to expect a one-to-one relationship between promises and practices, or simply that office holders behave that way "because that's the nature of politics," then one can gauge the cynicism of the modern scene. Has the noble art of political science been reduced to a Machiavellian notion of politics being the struggles for power, or any activity in relationship to power? If the very model or public image of the leader is tarnished by personal or public behavior demonstrating graft or corruption, why are such leaders even tolerated? It is suspected that the populace has become too disillusioned, too weary or too indifferent to perform their ethical imperatives: namely to vote the culprits out of office! Only then can there truly be hope in the process of democracy by indirect representation. The time has come to restore faith in the elective process so that the popularly held notion that "people run their government" can be enhanced.

Since taxes play a vital role in the services performed by the government, this issue is considered next.

The Issue of Taxation

Components of a Culture

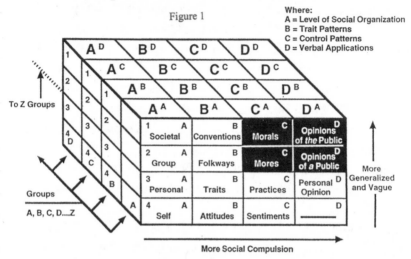

Figure 1

Where:
A = Level of Social Organization
B = Trait Patterns
C = Control Patterns
D = Verbal Applications

Adapted from The Shaping and Reshaping Forces of Acculturation: A Study of Risk, George Farrah © 1993, St. Cloud, MN.

3C
Practices

4C
Sentiments

If one were to carefully examine the volumes of history written by the eminent scholar, Arnold Toynbee, one would note two dominant themes in his methodology. These themes include the idea that the great civilizations have attributes of 1) challenge and 2) response. In particular, the concept of response entails to what degree a people can rise to a particular challenge. Without question, the challenge facing our nation today is coping with the enormous debt resulting from the war in Iraq and other military ventures.

Since the amenities of a high civilization requires loyal support in the form of taxes from its citizens, this process is a crucial challenge, because its ability to survive may depend on the nature of the response. For example, taxes make possible an array of services including free public education, police and fire protection, garbage disposal, sewers, partial or full support for its less fortunate citizens, and other important societal functions. In fact, taxes yield almost all of the revenues received by the local levels of government: federal, state or local. The exception to these latter sources involve funds received by borrowing. Increasingly, in this modern setting, there is the imperative that one pays taxes according to one's ability to pay. With the passage of time, the laws governing taxation have become unwieldy and complex, despite congressional efforts to simplify them.

Within the free enterprise system of the American Way of Life, there appears to be a critical balance among the factors of the laborer (i.e., wages), production sales (i.e., profit or loss), and supply and demand. At this historical stage, one crucial variable is the problem of inflation. This world-wide phenomenon is the catalytic agent that seems to pit unions against management, farmers against consumers; that cruelly eats away at the savings of retired persons; and that causes world prices and currencies to become unstable.

The post-war years of 1946 to approximately 1972 provided a period where the national economy expanded, and, thus, the tax base also expanded. It was a time of great optimism. It was a time of (nearly) full employment. It was a time of great investment and expansion by industry and business in diverse fields, both here and abroad. In fact, it was a time when the idea of economic progress, of continued growth, had no limits. Faith in economic expansion, with its various indices of growth, was really a way of life; even though there were ominous signs that the giant bubble–this illusion of unbridled progress–was about to burst!

Economists during the twentieth century have their own theories about taxation and its function. From John Maynard Keynes to John Kenneth Galbraith, and from Robert L. Heilbroner to Alan Greenspan, there have been diverse and often conflicting ideas about the role of government in free, private enterprise, international trade, tariffs, and a host of other issues. Yet, they agree that the finances of government compel the leadership to get the money needed in the cheapest and fairest way possible. Ideally, the process should not be too heavy or burdensome to any group, but, rather, it should be proportional to income—at a higher rate on higher incomes.

Therefore most Western countries have moved in the direction of developing ethical imperatives of political-social reform. One finds that taxes provide generous expenditures for the benefit (i.e., in other special grants or entitlements) of people with low incomes. In fact, both the federal and state governments, as reflected in tax measures, have followed the idea of social reform and the intended purpose of changing society in one way or another. For example, there have been progressive income taxes; sales and poll taxes; heavy taxes on cigarettes and liquor to discourage injurious or bad habits; corporate income taxes; severance taxes designed to save natural resources; hunting and fishing license as a source of tax revenue; and taxes on large chain department stores.

The justice for any system of taxation depends very much on factors beyond the control of people or groups. In other words, what is "just" for one group may well be "unjust" for another. Whenever a tax revision does occur, new rates have a way of upsetting the habits or practices that people seem to have acquired with "old" taxes in terms of their expectations and spending patterns. Moreover, in the world of everyday commerce, some businesses and some kinds of property will experience a tax increase. Thus, some people will gain via the reduction, which others will lose—through no fault of their own.

Much has been written about theories regarding the apportionment of the tax burden. One notes a range of theories, but the rationale for these theories and their application to various tax situations is beyond the intent or scope of this chapter.

What is significant, however, is that throughout the centuries of Western civilization, one finds that the issues of taxation are a critical catalyst for political and social action. Often, among other complex societal issues, it becomes the economic straw that breaks the camel's back, much as the "Boston Tea Party" became a rallying point for our own Revolutionary War. For example, some years ago there was the attempt in California to rebel against excessive–and from their viewpoint, unreasonable–taxation via "Proposition Thirteen."

However, the price of civilization, via taxes, rural and urban, can be expensive and requires a bureaucracy to achieve higher levels of existence. In Western civilization, there exists many levels of financial stratification. In America, one finds such descriptive terms as middle class, upper-middle class, lower-middle class, etc. In contrast, many European countries refer to the dominant group as "The Middle Way," when the proportion of rich and poor are relatively smaller than the majority group of citizens.

Consider that, within the macro and micro environments of the social class structure in America, the heavy burden of taxes has fallen on the dominant middle class. Even in Europe, one speaks of the monetary encroachments made on "The Middle Way" as taxes soar with increased social services.

Despite these graduations by income, Americans tend to identify with the middle class or "Middle Way," regardless of a high or low income. The concept of the so-called "life style" or pattern of living might be at great variance with the strict identification along financial status. Thus, a person with less financial resources may have reading and musical tastes that differ considerably from the more fortunate, but this difference does not prevent him/her from <u>identifying</u> with the dominant group.

Yet, the ethical imperative of spreading the wealth has become a practice, a way of life for the millions who enjoy a comparative high standard of living–especially by world standards. However, despite this blessing of economic abundance, there are ominous signs that the challenge to maintain this system has become enormous.

For example, the post-war years of 1946 to approximately 1972 provided a period where the national economy expanded, and, in turn the tax base also expanded. It was a time of great optimism. It was a time of (nearly) full employment. It was a time of great investment and expansion by industry and business in diverse fields, both here and abroad. In fact, it was a time when the idea of economic progress, of continued growth, had no limits. Faith in economic expansion, with its various indices of growth to measure progress, was really a way of life, even though there were ominous signs that the giant bubble–this illusion of unbridled progress–was about to burst!

It suddenly became painfully apparent that there was, in America, a decline or demise of many key industries: textiles, steel, and automobile production were prime examples of this economic deterioration. Yet, within the highly complex structure of Western economies, where international business is highly competitive and vital, the relationship between taxes and the economy of any particular country is both powerful and delicate.

For example, the twentieth century phenomenon of inflation, of debt-ridden budgets, and of unfavorable balances of trade are intimately associated with taxes. If a government elects to increase taxes in order to curb inflation, then it also runs the risk of discouraging investment by corporations or individuals. However, a more timely method employed by the Federal Reserve System is to increase the interest rate to curb inflation or to decrease it in order to stimulate the economy when necessary.

If a government chooses to impose import taxes on incoming goods to offset unfair trade practices by a foreign country, then it also risks a fruitless and unproductive trade war. One can immediately see that the economic weapon of taxes is powerful, but, at the same time, the relationship of that action to any given problem is delicate: an entire series of events, much like the domino effect, is set into motion.

Before moving on to the last section of this chapter, the relationship–an oblique one in most cases–of speculation to taxation deserves some treatment because it remains a lurking, important factor.

Just as capitalism became the life blood and economic catalyst for the Western countries, so the method of speculation has been the prime motive for development and expansion. In particular, American history abounds with themes of the relationship of speculation to economic growth. For example, consider the western movement and the role of speculation in land use, industrial development, and the building of railroads. Thus, the speculative characteristics inherent in the movements or economic matter of the West are reflected at various stages in their histories.

With the nineteenth and twentieth century revolutions in technology and communications, speculation–especially since money achieved the status of a <u>virtue</u> comparable and ranked with other virtues–took on new forms of risk in almost all ventures of the American Way of Life. Business, then, ceased to be just an occupation which had to be conducted in accordance with a moral code: it was now a part of that code in a money-driven marketplace.

However, in the countless ventures where speculation produced either profits or eventual bankruptcy, one virtual factor of the economy was the farmer, and his unique circumstances in the phenomenon of speculation required special comment—a topic considered earlier in this book.

Generally, if speculation produced greater profits, it also produced greater revenue for government in the yield of various kinds of taxes. Since most money-making is characterized by being impersonal, the kind of speculation employed was also impersonal. It mattered little that one could speculate by buying a piece of city or county property, letting it remain vacant for years, and then selling the land for a handsome profit. Taxes for that individual or corporation would be the same as one who had a comparable land value but speculated on a building, product, etc., but failed miserably: that company was taxed as much or more because of its increased value.

If speculation is the necessary handmaiden of investment, then one must distinguish between productive and unproductive speculation. In the latter example of vacant land remaining idle until "the price is right," this kind of speculation is defined as unproductive. On the other hand when effort of some kind—construction in the example of idle land—is expended to maintain or improve personal property, that effort may be characterized as productive speculation. In similar manner, when a farmer plants his seeds, the resultant crops after a season of growth is a dynamic form of productive speculation.

Obviously, one should be permitted to speculate in any form, manner, style, amount, etc., regardless of how one defines the process! Investment remains the core element in the capitalistic system and it should always be encouraged. However, and it is the crucial point being made here: if one chooses to speculate in the unproductive mode, taxes for that individual or corporation should be at a higher rate than one who has the ethical imperative to improve his investment. Imagine the ripple effect such a distinction would have on the economic endeavors of individuals and companies struggling to survive in the American

Way of Life! Imagine the stimulation in morale and effort, really a "people renewal" program, productive speculation would have on millions of city dwellers, knowing that their efforts in self-improvement would not result in an increase in taxes. Rather, and it is implicit in this latter statement, there is the possibility that city governments might even <u>reduce</u> taxes for such home or property improvement!

At this historical junction, where expressway canyons of concrete separate huge clusters of disadvantaged citizens from the more affluent suburbs, the property tax base has eroded. It would seem prudent for all levels of government to create programs for self-improvement, as several cities across America have already done. Again, improvement should not result in an automatic tax increase for the property owner. Undeniably, home or business properties warrant an increased valuation in terms of the improvement achieved, and such an increase in value should be welcome to the owner. Eventually, because of improved or additional services provided by the local government or school district, individuals would have to pay additional taxes. Nevertheless, the incentives to create more productive speculation should be encouraged in our way of life. Generally, most citizens understand the relationship between taxes and governmental services—as long as the system is fair and equitable.

Among the important economic institutions in America and the West is the Stock Market, because tax laws are intimately associated with speculation in the market—especially profits or losses on investments made. Most speculation there may be characterized as productive in the positive effects resulting from investments. For newer or older corporations, it is a critical source of money for expansion or other economic plans for operation or development. However, quite clearly, not all stock investments lead to capital improvements—most are just paper transfers! The importance of the stock market to our everyday thinking about speculation is enormous. One can gauge this pervasive phenomenon by the available number of indices describing the Market's ability. These indices include "economic indicators, trends, averages of the major stocks," etc., etc.

The magnitude of stock that exchanges hands every day, in terms of profit or loss, is staggering! With the advent of a complex and efficient technology, all aspects of buying and selling stock, from the local investment broker to the central stock exchange, the computer has become indispensable. The rapidity of millions of transactions has created problems in the process of making the trading of stocks easier to handle. For example, computers are programmed to buy or sell automatically, so at this stage of the sale the transaction becomes impersonal and at the mercy of technology.

One only has to observe fluctuations in the stock market here or abroad to realize how intricate, dependent, and intermeshed are the markets of the Western world. Whatever happens on the New York exchange on any given day has immediate repercussions on stock exchange centers in London, Amsterdam, Frankfort, Paris, Stockholm, Tokyo, and vice versa! The effects are instant and dramatic: within minutes, millions of shares are traded and profits or losses are realized by the fortunate and the not so fortunate respectively.

Another development has had a profound effect on the market: the behavior of certain individuals, who, for whatever reasons of hostility or friendliness, make it their business to "take over" a corporation. Amply justified with rational arguments of "creating a more efficient company" or simply "to increase the profits," any corporation can become fair game or the target. It matters little that many "blue chip" corporations have long-standing traditions, often involving family ownership. It matters little that these same corporations have commitments to the community, to their employers, and to maintaining a tax base for the local and state governments. While it is true that a new ownership would not necessarily alter the latter facts, and would help to "weed out" the weaker corporation, the ethical imperatives of very high standards of conduct permeated the behavior of those who were the stock market "regulars." Whether these same high standards are still the rule, is open to question.

Most important, where the return on one's investment was under the magic spell of security and confidence that faith in the "blue chip" stock has gradually deteriorated with the disclosures of various scandals. One could no longer depend on the reputation and established record of an old family business, where ethical imperatives governed the "rules of the game," and normally (and there were exceptions, of course) individuals followed those rules–largely unwritten because they were the normal practices of doing business on Wall Street.

In the daily interaction and contacts that are made between individuals and groups which result in success or failure, the aspects of leadership, power, and authority are vital factors. An analysis of these factors is considered next.

Elements of Leadership, Power, and Authority: Masters of Promise

Components of a Culture

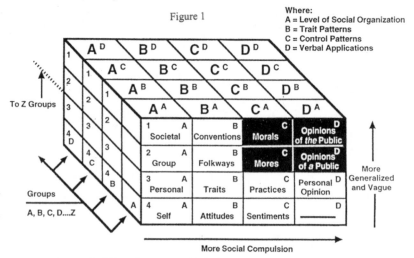

Figure 1

Where:
A = Level of Social Organization
B = Trait Patterns
C = Control Patterns
D = Verbal Applications

Adapted from The Shaping and Reshaping Forces of Acculturation: A Study of Risk, George Farrah © 1993, St. Cloud, MN.

All Components Are Involved

In my experiences both in our country and in Europe, it became clear to me that the patterns of leadership, power, and authority vary tremendously from country to country. These differences will result from the prevailing conventions, practices, sentiments, folkways, morals, mores, and the other cultural components depicted above. Although an analysis of these three elements reveals that they are closely related, each concept should be further analyzed to describe its impact on our democratic form of government typical in Western societies. A great deal has been written about these three components; in fact the literature abounds with information relating to the numerous points of entry that are possible for exercising each of them. However, for this particular section, in addition to treating them within the context of organizational behavior, the focus here also relates to a more general application to the areas of government, economics, and education—aspects of the American Way of Life.

For the element of leadership, one finds that there are over three hundred fifty theories about what leadership <u>should be</u> or what it <u>is</u>. It should also be noted that this latter contrast corresponds to the cultural components of Morals and Mores in Column C of the above illustration. This portrait of leadership involves the factors of time, energy, space and the priorities in response to the process of shaping and re-shaping.

Therefore, as a dynamic process of coping, interacting, and applying, leadership can take many forms. For example, as a vital link to cultural vitality, leadership provides the impetus for the transformation of values. Yet, despite this multitude of theories regarding leadership—at any level of social organization—can yield a wealth of information about good or poor leadership. For example, by his or her own example, to what extent does the style of leadership empower those who follow with the opportunity to grow, to learn, or to excel at a given task? In the world of economics or business, how does the leader motivate and inspire those in the workforce to achieve a mission or necessary goal? In education how do administrators and teachers apply the goals of their board of education in order to maximize talent and enrich the acculturation process of young people and children? In government, from the lowest to the highest levels, from mayors, governors to congressional representatives and senators, how well do these leaders truly represent their constituents?

While these questions could be extended to include a myriad of organizations in our infrastructure, wherever leadership is effective in achieving the necessary goals, the answers to the aforesaid questions are readily apparent—they can be found in two human practices and sentiments: truthfulness and a purity of purpose. Fortunately, as our great country emerged in its leadership role among countries of the world, it was due to not only "Yankee Ingenuity," but also to the vision of our many exemplary leaders, and their ethical imperatives! From the political leaders to the captains of industry, with the tremendous output of goods and services, America was, and continues to be, a model for the world!

If one examines the practices inherent in the different styles of leadership that result in successful endeavors, the concepts of transformation and transaction are extremely important. For example, in the case of transactional leadership, the rationale and sentiments for it involves the two factors of contingent reward, and management by exception. Whereas contingent reward leadership is regarded as an active and agreed- upon exchange (i.e., of objectives) between leaders and followers, the resultant rewards are a form of recognition from the leader for the accomplishment of the objective. In addition to this recognition, there may also be bonuses or merit rewards. The crucial aspect here really is job performance.

Thus, if the leader clearly specifies the objectives that followers are to achieve, then rewards will be given for satisfactory performance. In this instance, one may infer that the more congruent the objectives or goals are between the leader and her or his subordinates the greater the possibility of achieving mutually agreed-upon objectives. As a result, this process or practice is enhanced by further communications between the leader and followers, where formal or informal contracts specify the terms of the agreement for any work done, as well as the rewards to follow.

Most important, the effective leader knows how to model the behavior desired so that he or she can live up to the role expectations of the followers. However, if and when the leader—for whatever the reason—fails to fulfill these expectations, motivation suffers. There could also be a diminished feeling of trust and respect for this leader. In connection with the elements of trust and a purity of purpose, it was James MacGregor Burns who stated that the "pervasiveness" of transformational leadership affects many societal roles such as teachers, parents, and peers as well as preachers and politicians. Here, with his idea of trust, Burns reiterates the important principles of leadership stated earlier; namely, a purity of purpose and truthfulness. These human characteristics are the directional compass point in the process of transformational leadership.

In terms of the second factor of transactional leadership, there is the more passive style of management by exception. The dominant themes here rely on observing mistakes and not intervening until something has gone wrong. In passing, one notes that this passive style of management (i.e., "do things right" or there is intervention) is quite different in meaning than the leadership style which is dynamic and active (i.e., "do the right things"). This comparison by W. G. Bennis is an excellent contrast between the two styles of leadership, transactional in the former instance, and transformational in the latter.

Therefore, management by exception is contextual in nature. For example, if something is going well, leave it alone! However, if the "know how" suffers or things are not done right, then it is time to take action to correct the situation or process. This kind of emphasis might be appropriate or efficient for more immediate goals or tasks, but, eventually, if the process of change and long-range planning are neglected, management by exception could well lower standards of excellence! These aforesaid practices are typical of what has now become commonly known as "micro-management," and, thus, it contributes to our (formerly) cutting edge or avante-gardé style of leadership.

Without doubt, transformational leadership is a different philosophy. Within this concept, there are these attributes of shaping and reshaping. As defined earlier, values then become the mainspring by which an individual is able to cope, to interact, and to apply those necessary elements of acculturation. Herein, if one examines this concept currently known as leadership, training, and so on, one recognizes the weakness: the lack of an integrative approach which can be dynamic, active, and personal. The reader will note that, in order to avoid passivity, coping, interacting and applying are active verbs. In university founded longitudinal studies involving data-generated information from nationwide and European samples, beginning in 1977 and continuing to the present, I identified these three verbs to describe an aspect of the reshaping process for the transformation of values. Therefore, it is incumbent upon those who deal with leadership and values to maximize the talents of others so that their experiences are meaningful in their lives.

Since transformational leadership is a dynamic process involving change of some kind, one begs the question: What is it that the leader transforms as a shaping force in the micro environment? To the extent that he or she models this type of leadership, is it one or more of the following qualities that are transformed: trust, commitment, integrity, credibility, charisma, inspiration, influence, or purity of purpose? If indeed these personal qualities can be transformed, then the latter may act in concert to produce a difference. For example, if the leader transforms commitment, then it can be inferred that commitment produces a difference in credibility and *vice versa*!

Suppose for instance, that the shaping force happens to come from the mass media (where there is often distortion in meaning), how does the individual transform that information so he or she can reshape the phenomena for meaning to him or her? There are also the various obvious distortions that come from political leaders who use their campaigns for shaping public opinions. It is crucial for the person involved to have the abilities and skills that are inherent in the interaction process to reshape this phenomena also. Within this context, the individual, often caught in a maze of conflicting values, is unable to deal with change, stress or unfavorable conditions.

Since both power and authority are key elements in the shaping forces of our society, their purpose and use are matters of vital concern. It is generally agreed that power is the ability of a leader to influence a group or another person. In this respect, there may be a considerable distance between those leaders who have great power and those who follow with little or no power. For example, in a political campaign, one has the power to make promises regarding some issue of concern to his/her constituents. However, unfortunately, once elected this master of promises had no intention of keeping the campaign promises. There are other misuses of power and authority far too numerous to describe in this section and they are common themes for numerous scholars in the field. In passing, it should be noted that at all levels of social organization, from government to the world of business, the judicial use of power and authority are necessary elements for the very survival of the American Way of Life, especially the aspect of authority. For example, one important characteristic that authority has in our democratic form of government is the quality of <u>protection</u> for its citizens. This protection is central and inherent in the mission or work of teachers, those in law enforcement, religious leaders and a host of other fields. In achieving their mission, the <u>position of power</u> they hold ensures their legitimacy, earned respect, and success in decision-making activities. However, and it is a most important consideration, there is a <u>very thin line</u> that separates power and authority from those who use their leadership role for purposes of <u>control</u>! Tragically, our history abounds with those leaders or individuals who deliberately cross that line to achieve their hidden agendas!

Ideally, while the process of transformational leadership does not automatically guarantee success in reaching a goal, its emphases on truthfulness, purity of purpose, and empowering others to maximize their talents has tremendous potential in these uncertain times of risk and danger. It transcends an allegiance to a political party, gender, age, location, or ethnic origin. Finally, that there is a crucial difference between transactional and transformational leadership. Very briefly, many astute scholars as Bass, Burns, Covey, Tracey, Yammarino, Zaleznick and so many others who cannot be included in this limited space have observed or tested the dominant themes of transformational leadership. For example, they discovered that this type of leader can broaden and thus maximize the talents of their subordinates by generating awareness and acceptance among the subordinates toward the purpose and mission of the group. They know that this unique leader can motivate others to go beyond their own self-interests for the good of the group.

In order to provide a vivid illustration of the tremendous potential of transformational leadership and its effects on values, it is now appropriate to consider the example that was set by Gandhi—leader *par excellence!*

Mahatma Gandhi has become known to millions around the world for his purity of purpose and dedication to a cause— perhaps the mainspring to any transformation. However one may ask, how is it that this shy, awkward, at one time lawyer, employed basic values as a new vision for India? Imagine this eventual leader turning his back on his modestly wealthy family and comfortable situation in order to reach out to the teaming millions: the homeless, destitute, and untouchables. A freelance, political journalist, Vincent Shehan became acquainted with Gandhi and later wrote a biography about him. The facts or events presented here about Gandhi's life and political struggles were extracted from Shehan's masterful account.

Gandhi's ethical imperatives were rooted in the great Hindu poem "Bhagavad-Gita" and the Sermon on the Mount. One imperative was most important to him: the value of being good and of living the good life. In this instance "good" for Gandhi involved other key imperatives. For example, there was the Sanskrit words for voluntary sacrifice which Gandhi's cousin Maganlal had used: *sat* or truth, and *agraha*, which is firmness or force. By combining, for the very first time, these potentially powerful and dynamic concepts, Gandhi converted them into one expression—*satyagraha*!

In setting the transformational stage for the masses in India—both Hindu and Moslem—Gandhi's style of leadership provided an easier, more comprehensible way of understanding his struggle for freedom. Imagine the tremendous impact of these imperatives and ideas; they eventually took root and grew, and grew, and grew! With the liberation of India, pax Britannia, "where the sun never set on the Union Jack," would never be the same again.

Of course, this independence was his ultimate achievement. There were other values that contributed to this aforesaid achievement. For example, as a model for others to follow, he believed that a purity of purpose, unadulterated by ego or self-centeredness, was a crucial responsibility for the leader. Thus, via his frequent fasting in order to achieve a goal, this "self-purification" in turn was also regarded as the purification by his thousands of followers. Therefore, if Gandhi fasted, they, too, at his signal and appropriate time, also fasted.

His imperatives and achievements in this transformation process are valuable guidelines for those of us living in a world of uncertainty. In addition to the aforesaid value of *satya* or truth, Gandhi was also motivated by the value of *brahmacharya*, which is self-control or chastity.

At this stage of our history, the first decade of the twenty-first century, the implication of Gandhi's values for transformational leadership are profound. Most importantly, in retrospect, if Gandhi could accomplish so much with so little, how is it that leaders today, with many greater resources, experience difficulty in achieving their goals? Is it any wonder that Lord Halifax, who personally dealt with Gandhi as viceroy from England, had the highest regard for him, characterizing Gandhi as "the little man" who had never broken a promise.

Therefore, there can be little doubt of the dynamic relationship that values have with commitment and credibility, especially in that relationship between the leader and those who follow. Therein is the crucial factor: the leader is <u>*supra personal*, beyond his or her own intrinsic, immediate needs, and the latent, extrinsic objective is most paramount.</u>

The living proof of Gandhi's transformation can be seen in the revolutionary model of Martin Luther King in his policy of nonviolence. Quite clearly, in a transformation process, Gandhi's leadership—often in the face of self-doubt and challenges from his adversaries–produced a difference in credibility and commitment.

It is evident from this illustration of Gandhi that he entertained many self-doubts regarding his own efficacy in helping his fellow man, Hindu or Moslem. However, he treated both with the same compassion; his ultimate success could not be divorced from these actions. Gandhi and those possessing this magnificent vision tell us that this is not a historical oddity, a product of the moment, or a passing fad. Historically, the leaders, dreamers, and rebels have transformed organizations, nations, and peoples with the power of their values and vision.

In Part II, the implications of the ideas and materials presented in these four chapters are provided.

EPILOGUE

PART II: SUMMARY AND CONCLUSIONS

For those of us who have become conditioned to the new meanings or interpretation to the concept of culture, I selected eight topics for Chapter One to describe how this vital aspect of our West has been atomized. Tragically, as its meaning changed or became distorted, the sixteen components have not been given the emphases necessary for cultural vitality. Of these components, the distance between morals and mores reflect the pattern and quality of leadership—especially the ethical choices that leaders make in the process of shaping these morals and mores. Therefore, the components provide a clearer view of societal and organizational indices and are critical points of entry for our serious problems.

* * * * * * * * * * * * * * * * * * * *

In terms of the future of our American Way of Life, education has come to the forefront in the process of acculturation. Unfortunately, at all societal levels, it has become so politicized that the average American citizen has difficulty in separating the wheat from the chaff. The citizen has been bombarded with a number of "quick fixes" for long standing problems confronting our communities—especially those students who are at-risk both in our deteriorated inner cities and rural areas of America. For example, the "No Child Left Behind" program launched by the national leadership has been a tremendous disappointment to our educational leaders and teachers as well as parents. At best, these were good intentions made by politicians in order to make improvements in the educational lives of children. However, at worst, in order to achieve the goals of this program, funding was totally inadequate. Here, again, as in so many instances, the gulf between the morals (i.e., the "should be" in education) and the mores (i.e., the actual system) has to be closed. Apparently, in the shaping forces of the acculturation process, where children and youth spend considerable time in school, education is a dominant force and influence. Yet, paradoxically, while the truly professional educators—those fine leaders and teachers who are committed to enhancing the lives and future of their students—have the knowledge and ability to solve many serious issues confronting them, they lack the power to resolve these issues. Conversely, those leaders or citizens outside of the profession, often lacking the knowledge but having the power, affect educational changes which prove to be deleterious or ineffective for the improvement of schools.

With the continuous attacks that have been made on public schools and the profession itself by various groups or individuals, it is not surprising to learn that teachers' morale has sunk to a low ebb. Moreover, it is little wonder that our most capable teachers, both young women and men, are leaving the profession in droves—tragically, only after a few years of experience in schools across America.

Fortunately, many communities are learning that, with the right choices and their involvement in school life, it is possible to enhance the role and morale of teachers.

* * * * * * * * * * * * *

The recent innovations and methods of disseminating information have profoundly affected the shaping and reshaping process of opinions—especially the opinions of a public, in contrast to opinions of the public.

With the third topic or section dealing with "Articulate Propaganda versus Sensory Reactions," media sources have ranged from more formal to less formal sources. Those networks and other sources have made it possible to influence and to shape opinions often at odds with the particular public they serve. Despite the tremendous advances in computer technology and the great impact it has had on all phases of our daily lives, there must be a constant awareness of the immediate advantages versus the latent possibilities inherent in the choices one makes. These choices center on data and information—as though these advantages of immediacy were sufficient alone—are in considerable contrast to the higher levels of knowledge and wisdom. Therefore, our ability to recast the immediate choices into the latent future will depend largely on how well we cope, interact, and apply. Of these latter three, to lessen the chances of becoming a voiceless society, the frequency and degree of interaction are critical. The choices of more emphases on interaction will strengthen our cultural vitality.

* * * * * * * * * * * * * * * * *

As a social practice in Western and American ways of feeling, thinking, and acting, the family is a vital link to the group and other levels of social organization. Without any doubt whatsoever, the changing roles of the family structure, especially the practice of marriage, have been documented by experts in the field. A wealth of constructive information and knowledge has been developed by professionals such as religious leaders, psychiatrists, school counselors, sociologists, political leaders, and media commentaries or newspaper columnists. Most significant, regardless of the wisdom and knowledge gained from age-old morals, traditions and values of our multicultural heritage concerning marriage, certain ethical choices have been ignored or replaced with a neutral relativism. Unless wiser, more prudent choices or decisions are made about marriage, the family will continue to be at risk.

* * * * * * * * * * * * * * * * * *

There is a growing concern in America regarding the changes in our economy, particularly the commitment we have made to a global economy. This choice has been applauded as being advantageous in the long run for the United States. However, when one evaluates the consequences of this global emphases, there are many questions that deserve answers. For example, from the growing phenomenon of the economic choice of outsourcing, with the concomitant, tragic loss of thousands of jobs, wherein is the fairness or justice of this practice? What power does the average worker have—who continually struggles to make ends meet—to alter this great shift in jobs?

In terms of off-shoring forecasts, several estimates have been made concerning its impact on the U.S. jobs. According to the Forrester Report of November 11, 2002, it was stated that "Over the next 15 years, 3.3 million U.S. services industry jobs and 136 billion in wages will move offshore to countries like India, Russia, China, and the Philippines". Aided by the power of our government via free trade agreements, the American consumer has become accustomed to buying the vast number of items or goods that are being produced abroad—especially automobiles—and being shipped to America on ships or planes! What Americans are not accustomed to is the increasing number of jobs that have been eliminated.

Most important, since the basis of our economy has shifted its emphases to a service economy rather than production of goods, the loss of services to other countries will continue to escalate the loss of jobs in our country. This transfer of jobs to other countries will be a boost to their economies. However, one wonders if, under their governments, more employment will result in a higher standard of living for their citizens. Conversely, with these losses concerning our workers, it is almost a certainty that their incomes will be reduced accordingly and a lower standard of living will result.

In terms of such everyday items as shoes, clothing, and, a host of other products and services, particularly shoemakers and tailors, the time is ripe for <u>manufacturing</u> these items in greater quantities and provide more needed goods and services which can be produced or provided by American workers. As noted in an earlier chapter, in order to survive in a highly competitive global marketplace, many manufacturers resorted to the practice of outsourcing their products or services. At the same time, one suspects that seeking higher profits on a greater return on their investment, the ugly head of greed has affected the motivation for outsourcing. Therefore, for many corporations, it was not a grave matter of survival, but, rather, "get as much as you can while the getting is good!"

With the possibility of creating more jobs for our citizens, our economy will become stronger and confidence will be restored from this initiative for the workplace.

* * * * * * * * * * * * * * * *

The topics of health care and transportation are also issues and concerns of great significance to our future.

A special case was made for the increasing prevalence of diabetes, especially among children. From the research I did regarding type 2 diabetes among the population of our fifty states, there are encouraging developments concerning programs dealing with preventative measures or techniques.

For example, most recently, the American Diabetic Association created and chartered a new organization in order to cope with the problems of being overweight and obese. Since both of these problems can lead to type 2 diabetes, this organization is aptly designated as "Shaping America's Health" (i.e., SAH). With a strong emphases on prevention, a study will soon explore the metabolic effects of several dietary compositions. In particular, various dietary compositions will be explored in order to determine the effects of various dietary compositions on type 2 diabetes.

In passing, it should be noted that, in terms of the present quality of health care that Americans receive, it is "woefully mediocre." Regardless of income, race, or other characteristics, in a recent survey of almost 7,000 patients, it was reported that "patients received only 55 percent of recommended steps for top-quality care—and no group did much better or worse than that." As the percentages figure in Table 4 indicate, several characteristics (i.e., gender, age, race, and income) were considered. Therefore, the issue of health care should be a top priority item for our leadership personnel at all levels of government.

Then, along with health care, transportation also deserves immediate attention by decision makers at the national level. Despite the dedicated and visionary effort exerted by so many groups and individuals in many geographical regions of our country, change to more expedient ways of travel is painfully slow and involved. It is similar to trying to scratch one's initials on granite!

Without question, there is a need for balance among several alternatives for travel. Rather than our heavy dependence on automobiles and airplanes, there must be a shift in our habits to the advantages of travel by train and bus.

* * * * * * * * * * * * * * * *

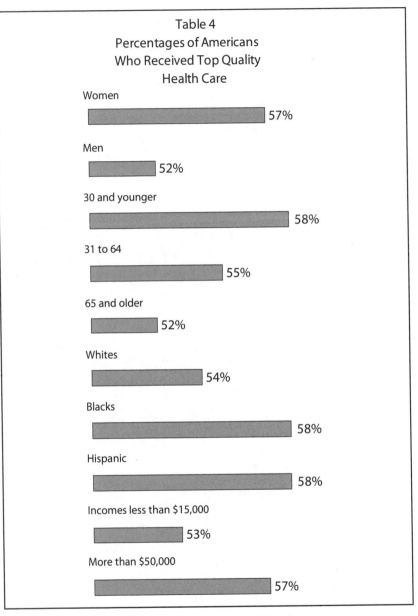

Table 4
Percentages of Americans
Who Received Top Quality
Health Care

Women
57%

Men
52%

30 and younger
58%

31 to 64
55%

65 and older
52%

Whites
54%

Blacks
58%

Hispanic
58%

Incomes less than $15,000
53%

More than $50,000
57%

Source: New England Journal of Medicine
Survey taken between October 1998 and August
2000 in 12 metropolitan areas from Boston to
Miami to Seattle.

Table 5

The Effects of Fertilizer and Fuel on Farm Income Between
the Years of 2003 and 2006

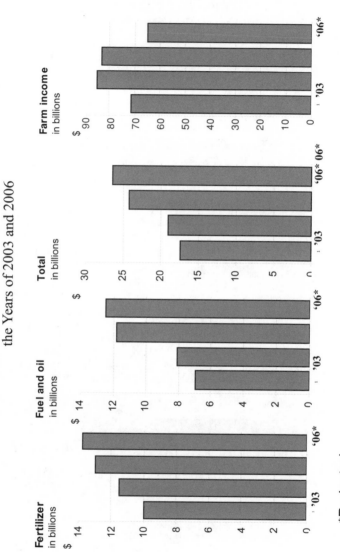

*Projected.

Source: U.S. Department of Agriculture

From Chapter 2, the focus and treatment of the existential topics related to meaning and identity, the shaping force of psychology helped to create three aspects of personality. Defined as coping, interacting, and applying, a better framework and understanding of values is possible.

Self-concept and motivation are important elements in the personality of the individual. While the former element involves self-adequacy and role expectations in <u>immediate</u> experiences or settings, the latter concerns the personal investment and goal needs of the person for the <u>latent</u> future. These elements of personality are affected by the shaping forces of society and the individual reshapes his/her responses to those forces in terms of coping, interacting, or applying.

It was during the Twentieth Century that the contributions of Freud, Jung, and others provided fresh insights to those forces that converge on the individual. The concepts of emotions, traits, attitudes and a host of other terms were enhanced by these two giants who made significant contributions to the understanding of our emotional and mental processes.

In terms of religious faith, if Christianity or other belief systems are to produce a positive difference, then the distance between cultural vitality and anemia must be bridged.

* * * * * * * * * * * * * * * * *

The dominant themes presented in Chapter 3 were culled from the interviews of three individuals from the northern part and one person from the central area of Minnesota. From the eleven generalizations given at the conclusion of the chapter, it is readily apparent that farming in general and dairy farms in particular are confronted with grave challenges. For example, there is an inverse relationship between the rising costs of fuel and fertilizer; and a decline in income for farmers here and elsewhere in our country. In other words, as expenses rise, income declines.

Tragically, as a result, thousands of farmers across our country are attempting to cope with their rapidly dwindling income or energy prices that affect their already narrow profit margin.

Here, in Benton County, Minnesota, there is a farmer who operates 1,000 acres of corn and owns 160 dairy cows. Imagine, his fuel bill rose 33 percent during the year 2005. Fortunately, in terms of his fertilizer bill, he was able to "lock in" on prices before they rose dramatically. In this exceptional case, his fertilizer bill increased by only 12 percent. In contrast, other farmers were less fortunate, because, in some instances, their fertilizer bills rose more than 50 percent! Table 5 summarizes the effects of these continuous, rising costs.

Since farmers will tell the interested person that they cannot rely on making a profit every year, the line or margin between success and failure over just a few years is very thin—it can be devastating to his future operation. Unlike other business alternatives, they cannot pass higher energy costs on to customers when the product leaves the farm. Again, unlike most businesses, it is the government that sets farm prices. Accordingly, when market prices fall below a certain level, farmers receive government subsidies.

Quite clearly, in terms of the future, there really is no easy, quick solution to remedy the farmer's plight—especially the many who are presently at great risk. Therefore, for our rural way of living and our vital dependence on food and dairy products, the choice we must make here is obvious and compelling: American farmers need our complete support. Otherwise, at some future time, one will ask, "What is a farm anyway?"

* * * * * * * * * * * * * * * *

There were several dominant themes in Chapter 4 related to the cultural components of morals, mores, practices, and sentiments in terms of our democratic practices.

First, central to the practices within a democracy, via their elected representatives, citizens run their government. Yet, it was shown that there is considerable variance between this ideal (i.e., the moral of "should be") and the actual practice (i.e., the mores or "is").

Second, central to the basic idea of a true democracy is <u>shared power</u>—a division of power which is not altered or changed by one party without the consent of the other party. It is really a delicate balance of power among the various levels of local government and our three federal branches of the executive, legislative, and judicial.

Finally, in order for a democracy to be effective in its operation, its elected officials must truly represent those citizens who voted for them rather than cater to other political agendas or influences.

With a national debt exceeding nine trillion dollars, the issue of taxation should be our highest priority. Unfortunately, at this writing our continued involvement in Iraq, and other areas of the Mid-East, over the past three years has diverted funds away from many of the necessary local and state governmental programs that deserve immediate attention. These are programs designed to assist our infrastructure, health care, veterans, the homeless, our suffering inner cities, and the rural areas of America. How long can these important programs be delayed?

* * * * * * * * * * * * * * * *

The reader will remember from the "Introduction" section of my book that I stated, "this work does not resemble the usual approach or format for a work of this nature." Therefore, the three appendices that follow this particular section provide important data, information, and knowledge that are related to certain issues such as the family, and farming. These issues are extracted topics presented in Chapters 1 through 4. Since the very concept of "Image" has meanings such as an imitation, a copy, a visual impression of something, or to reflect over a period of time, those images may become weakened by a number of shaping phenomena. Then over a period of time, because as humans we tend to forget events, persons, or situations, the images are less intense or disappear completely without a trace.

However, from reliable and valid information from the past based on several research grants which I was awarded during the early and mid-1970s, I obtained valuable information resulting from one nationwide project. Entitled <u>A Study of the American Way of Life</u>, it involved many of my colleagues at St. Cloud State University (SCSU), fifteen Minnesota Samples with 736 persons; fifteen Nationwide Samples with 736 persons; and a cross-section of professional, lay citizens, and students ranging from high school to university level from both Minnesota communities and locations elsewhere in the U.S. for a grand total of 1,472 persons who participated. Further details including the results from this research are given in Appendix A.

Immediately following this research noted above, I was again funded by the research committee at SCSU. The purpose was to conduct further research in Europe to replicate sampling done during my extended stay (i.e., the academic year of 1973-74) there. For this cross-cultural project, the methodology involved interviews with several key leaders in the fields of industry, commerce, and government in the countries of Germany and Spain. Ideally, additional sampling could have been done in other countries of Europe, but, because of limited funds, only the above countries could be involved. Fortunately, in addition to the interviews I did with leaders, questionnaires were also answered by 79 persons each from Germany and Spain.

With the above background and information from this longitudinal study of the American Way of Life, the results are presented in Appendix A.

Appendix A:

A Longitudinal Research Project Concerning the American Way of Life

Quite clearly, in our American Way of Life, the components of a culture described in Chapter 1 provide the organizational framework in which our precious democracy functions. Most important, in our democracy, individuals or members of a group are encouraged to express their sentiments, practices, beliefs, or life experiences. When these latter components are expressed in the form of verbal applications, they become <u>opinions of the public</u> or the <u>opinions of a public</u>.

Recent developments within the political, social, and economic context of America have discouraged or alarmed citizens in their quest for truth and understanding of their leaders and institutions. As described in previous sections, because of the confusion or distance between morals versus mores, there is a desperate need for better ways of assessing the general opinions of the American publics. Most important, there is also a critical need to transform or interpret the spectrum of objectives inherent in the American Way of Life without the distortions given by our mass media, groups, or persons who are only interested in promoting their own agendas!

Therefore, in retrospect, the conceptual framework utilized in my research involved a broad approach or design for the assessment of opinions regarding the American Way of Life. For example, the sampling included university students, parents, and other citizens throughout the state of Minnesota and elsewhere throughout the United States.

Concurrent with the sampling of fifteen locations in Minnesota which included a sample size of 736 were fifteen nationwide samples with a comparable size of 736. In terms of location, the latter samples ranged from Salem, Oregon to Charlotte, North Carolina. Included in the total sample of 1472 were individuals who were diverse in terms of age, occupation, gender, educational level, race, and geographic location.

Unique to the design was the comparative analysis between expert and lay opinions in seven arbitrary areas of the American Way of Life. The rationale for determining these seven areas were determined earlier in this book.

Moreover, the author limited the dimensions of the concept to include certain categories for detailed analysis. There are certain assumptions inherent in an investigation of this nature, and these are as follows:

1. That the category of government, viewed as a system of checks and balances, with appropriate divisions of power, forms one of the foundational pillars for the American Way of Life. In its brief history of two hundred years, despite internal and external perils, the American people have retained their confidence in this expression of self-determination, of free elections, and the entire process of arriving at some kind of consensus. Yet, even though the record has been overwhelmingly in favor of this unique federalism of United States, there have been disturbing signs that public confidence has been eroding in opinions held regarding governing officials, rather than about the system itself.

One notes considerable concern with such key issues as the role of political parties, freedom versus responsibility, and the alienation of thousands of individuals from the political process itself.

2. That the category of economics involves all aspects of the free enterprise system. In the American Way of Life, there appears to be a critical balance among the factors of the laborer, production, and supply and demand. One tremendously crucial variable at this historical moment are the problems associated with a global economy and the high cost of fuel. For example, this world-wide phenomenon is the catalytic agent that seems to pit unions against management, farmers against consumers; that cruelly eliminated thousands of jobs; and that caused world prices and currencies to become unstable.

Since this probe into a way of life is really addressed to middle-class America, one observes the great tragedy of millions of Americans who are not, for a variety of reasons, within the mainstream of this dominant middle-class. Ironically, it is suspected that most Americans identify themselves as belonging to this middle-class, even though their styles of life, income, and general values may vary tremendously!

3. That the category of science is the hallmark of some of the greatest contributions of Western individuals. Indeed, scientific technology has affected every mode of American life to contribute to its high standard of living. The awe-inspiring advances of the nineteenth and twentieth centuries have their roots in improved technology. Undoubtedly, there is a causal connection between the great acceleration of change within American practices and the advent of scientific technology. The vastness of the universe, subatomic physics, the quantum theory, non-Euclidean geometry, relativity, the advent of nuclear energy, bold ventures into space, and the new field of bio-mechanics are a few byproducts of this extensive scientific activity.

Yet, paradoxically, and almost as a caricature of religion, the belief that science is beneficial to man's happiness, or that it is wise to utilize science in controlling the environment, is now open to serious question. The conservation of energy, natural resources, and the utilization of the land and marine environments are critical areas of concern.

4. That the category of education may be the most crucial and controversial of all for America. Education in a modern industrial society has been so closely associated with political organization that its unique structure cannot be understood unless there is an understanding of its legal character. States have also delegated broad powers to local boards, and this power takes the form of "permissive laws" which describe and limit the many activities that local school districts may carry on under certain conditions. However, the American public school, conceptionally an impartial social agency, operates upon a consensus of public opinion. Hence, it is constantly vulnerable to polemics, and it seems destined to be subjected to criticisms by the sincere, intelligent citizen as well as to criticisms by the more radical and reactionary opinions.

Many of the current issues center on homogeneity versus heterogeneity of ability groupings, equal educational opportunity, methods of teaching the content areas, discipline, and the financing of schools, especially in view of decreasing enrollment patterns. Assuredly, the American public schools have been truly neighborhood institutions which serve as unifying elements for common core values. At the present time, with the multitude of problems faced by school districts across the nation, the very idea of free, public education is in jeopardy.

5. That the category of cultural aspects reflect important modes of living in the American Way of Life, especially the changing role of the family and the use of leisure time. This changing role mirrors changes in the morals and the mores of

the multitude of groups that comprise the population of the United States. In turn, the morals and the mores are intimately associated with the dynamic upheavals in matters political, economic, cultural, and intellectual which have characterized the twentieth century. For example, there have been devastating wars, revolutions, alarming examples of nationalistic and racial intolerance, and extensive experimentation in art and literature. There have been cyclical economic booms and depressions of unparalleled magnitudes. There have been various groups of civil rights and women's rights activists, anti-war activists, and those who have resisted ecological or environmental abuses. From these settings, these approaches, seeking new alternatives, seriously questioned time-honored traditions, institutions, and dogmas.

The very notion of "cultural pluralism" may be more idealistic than actuality. If one assumes that the latter concept depends on equal, proportional representation, input, or rights accorded to the ethnic groups of America, then, viewed from evidence to the contrary, cultural pluralism has not been achieved.

6. That the category of mass media has signified an extremely powerful influence on the thinking of various American publics. Within recent years, the medium of television has emerged as a dominant form of acquiring information or pure relaxation. Since the visual, dramatic, and emotional impact of television can produce many different kinds of effects, its content and format are of vital concern. However, the one effect which is crucial to the minds of young people is the effect that television has on imagery. For example, there may be considerable distortion to the process of imagination when, via a particular program, some writer has prescribed the content in such a way that the responses follow the predetermined pattern inherent in the plot, story, description, etc. The viewer cannot react directly to the stimuli presented, and, for clarifying (if it does occur!) an

interpretation, the young person must depend on the receptivity and availability of another mature viewer—hopefully a parent or adult who understands and who is interested!

On a broader plane, and of recent years, American newspapers have attempted to present the various publics with greater accuracy in reporting and for allowing more diverse opinions. One senses this diversity in the viewpoints expressed by the many syndicated columnists—from the more liberal to the more conservative opinions.

However, one also detects a growing suspicion about the purpose and effects of advertising. Although it is one of the pivotal points of the free enterprise system, the ultimate cost of advertising, which is borne by the consumer, is inextricably woven into the pricing system.

7. That the category of religion plays a dominant role in the American Way of Life. Having been founded on the principle of religious tolerance, there is a wonderful freedom to choose one's faith, whether it is faith in the invisible or faith in the visible.

This intervening variable of religion is the role of morality. If one inspects the current literature on the subject, one concludes that it has become a dominant concern for millions. Morality has been characterized as "no fault, deficit, or lax."

It seems that organized religion has borne the brunt of much criticism regarding changing values toward issues of morality. However, religious institutions, as all other institutions, are no better nor worse than the membership who comprise them.

* * * * * * * *

Having detailed the various parameters that constitute the American Way of Life as projected in this study, there remains the task of describing a few major aspects that transcend all categories.

Assuredly, as one reviews the assumptions made for government, economics, science, etc., it is discovered that there is considerable overlap of opinions or sentiments expressed toward these categories.

Apparently, the most dominant feeling throughout the nation—at least at this writing—is the feeling of uncertainty, which seems to permeate all levels of societal organization. For example there is the uncertainty caused by unemployment; there is the uncertainty of limited energy supplies; there is the uncertainty of America's role in international affairs; and there is the uncertainty of leadership qualities in all major institutions—especially the national leadership in government.

From this uncertainty and doubt, there has emerged a growing cynicism toward the leader, supposedly an expert in his field. Very few professions have escaped the avalanche of criticism or changes that have been hurled concerning the efficacy of the leader or professional person. Of course, in view of the recent high level of national scandals, some of the criticism is well-deserved. However, much as a disease that rages from one part of the body to another, the cynicism and latent hostility toward experts in general should serve as a note of warning to those interested in enhancing the American Way of Life. A growing mistrust by lay publics—from service-related to industrial or commercially related professionals—is evident in all sectors of the country. From the dedicated medical doctor who, at every turn, faces the prospect of a malpractice suit to the equally dedicated teacher who, with declining enrollments faces great uncertainty, are now highly suspect by many lay publics. The cynicism and mistrust seems to thrive on the notion that the exception (i.e., inefficient teacher or doctor) proves the rule! The battle cry of the cynic is summed up in the phrase "No Way!"

Yet, the very basis of leadership rests on the assumption of some kind of expertise in a given field, of an art with a scientific basis. There can be little doubt to the assertion that it is the leader who helps to "set the tone" for the morals of a people, whatever the given category for application.

* * * * * * * * * *

Most important, in terms of the research that was accomplished concerning the "American Way of Life," by June 15, 1977, the results from the Minnesota and nationwide samples had been compiled and published. There were three volumes: Volume I involved 'Theory, Method, and Interpretation'; Volume II included the 15 Minnesota Samples; and Volume III, the Nationwide Samples. In all, these three volumes totaled 488 pages!

Since a detailed analysis of these three volumes is beyond the scope of this book, only the highlights or salient features of this research will be presented in the pages that follow.

Specifically, the objectives of this research probe were:

1. To determine whether there were common core values (or the nature of congruency in values) among various groups or publics.

2. To replicate a pilot study involving samples from Minnesota and other locations throughout the United States.

3. To utilize an advisory committee from various publics (i.e., legislators, religious leaders, League of Women Voters, artists, etc.) to act as seven different panels in their areas of expertise as described below:

Area	Composition (N = 88)	Number
3.1 Government	Legislators; conservatives and liberals (i.e., 5 each)	10

3.2 Economics	Professors of Economics	3
3.3 Science	Professors of Science (3) Professors of Industry (3)	6
3.4 Education	Superintendents (6), Principals (12), Teachers (27), and Professors (2)	47
3.5 Cultural Aspects	League of Women Voters (4), Professors of Liberal Arts (5) and the Fine Arts	9
3.6 Mass Media	Professors of Communication	5
3.7 Religion	Protestant ministers (4) Catholic priests (4)	8

(It should be noted that, in selecting the experts for each of the above areas, the author selected only the designated chairperson of each, who in turn, choose the remaining persons in the appropriate panel.) The numbers are arbitrary and deliberately vary in size to determine any effects with different numbers in the lay publics tested.

4. To develop scaled profiles between a group designated as the experts (i.e., the morals) versus those identified as lay (i.e., the mores).

5. To assess the opinions of lay publics toward the American Way of Life in terms of such characteristics as sex, age, occupation, and geographic location.

6. To develop computerized data banks of the opinions indicated by various students (i.e., from junior high to the university level), parents, and other citizens in Minnesota and elsewhere in the United States.

7. To determine possible areas for the strengthening of citizenship in the social science curriculum.

In the next section, the author presents several techniques for achieving the aforesaid goals.

- Sampling Techniques

    1. Since the administration of the questionnaire was governed by the willingness of individuals to participate, simple random sampling was done in terms of sex, age, and occupation.

    2. The majority of sampling and testing was accomplished by persons other than the author. Some stratification occurred by the designation of certain regional locations throughout the United States.

        Key individuals, schools, institutions of higher learning from both Minnesota and elsewhere agreed to participate, and a total of 30 samples was involved. See Figure 5 for the Nation-Wide Distribution.

    3. An independent research project at New Hope, Minnesota afforded a comparison of all categories except Cultural Aspects, which was modified to emphasize the category of Education.

    4. Special attention was given to three different groups of Experts in Education to determine the extent of agreement between them. The agreement between certain lay publics, representing different parts of the country, was also compared.

- Analyses of Data

    The statistical treatment included these procedures:

    1. Analysis of means and variance.

    2. The development of profiles to test the homogeneity or congruency of agreements among various sets of publics versus the experts. Furthermore, the rationale to be tested

Figure 5

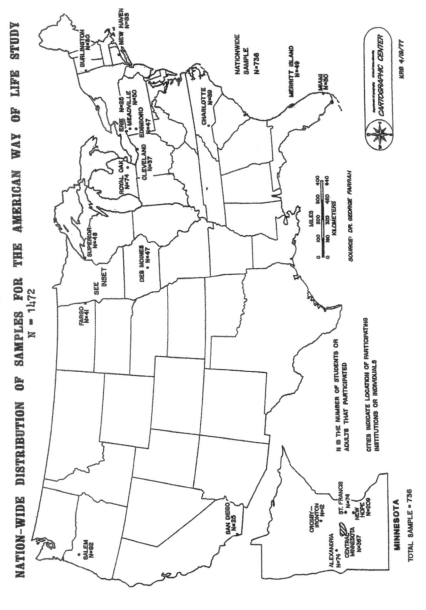

NATION-WIDE DISTRIBUTION OF SAMPLES FOR THE AMERICAN WAY OF LIFE STUDY

N = 1472

NATIONWIDE SAMPLE N=736

MERRITT ISLAND N=49

MIAMI N=50

CHARLOTTE N=50

NEW HAVEN N=85

BURLINGTON N=50

ERIE N=85
MEADVILLE N=50
EDINBORO N=47

CLEVELAND N=37

ROYAL OAK N=74

SUPERIOR N=48

SEE INSET

DES MOINES N=47

FARGO N=41

SALEM N=92

SAN DIEGO N=25

MILES
100 200 300 400
KILOMETERS
160 320 480 640

SOURCE: DR. GEORGE FARRAH

N IS THE NUMBER OF STUDENTS OR ADULTS THAT PARTICIPATED

CITIES INDICATE LOCATION OF PARTICIPATING INSTITUTIONS OR INDIVIDUALS

CROSBY— IRONTON N=74

ST. FRANCIS N=74

NEW HOPE N=209

ALEXANDRIA N=74

CENTRAL MINNESOTA N=367

MINNESOTA

TOTAL SAMPLE = 736

CARTOGRAPHIC CENTER

KRB 4/18/77

involved this logical sequence, which tested the statistical hypotheses of <u>relatedness</u>:

<u>Hr</u> (research hypothesis): that the use of the questionnaire produced differences among the various publics versus experts, especially in terms of certain population characteristics.

Hw (working hypothesis): that the use and comparison of these profiles and other statistical techniques produced differences in publics versus experts and in the characteristics of sex, age, occupation, and geographical location.

<u>Ho</u> (null hypothesis): that there were no significant differences among the various publics versus experts, and in the characteristics of sex, age, occupation, and geographical location.

3. Coding manuals and data banks for computerized treatment, storage, and retrieval were utilized.

4. Sectional summaries provided descriptive findings concerning the homogeneity versus the heterogeneity of the model and the population.

5. A content analysis of the Major Disciplines for the social sciences was made and compared to the items of the questionnaire. This analysis provided the degree of relationship between the results from the questionnaire and the content in the social studies (i.e., grades K-12).

As described earlier in Chapter 1—in fact, it was in the very first pages—the development of a questionnaire for the American Way of Life (i.e., AWOL) was initiated over forty years ago. Since the validity and reliability of the items selected would determine the credibility of the questionnaire, considerable time and effort were given to these two vital indices.

— Validity and Reliability

During the spring quarter of 1963, the original categories and items for the questionnaire were formulated at Wayne State University, Detroit, Michigan. The author, who was then on the part-time graduate staff at the aforesaid university, obtained the cooperative assistance of numerous professors (in appropriate fields of specialties), and a team of graduate students.

Basically, the initial step for validation was to determine the types of categories which would adequately describe the American Way of Life. Ultimately, while admittedly quite arbitrary, it was agreed to include the categories of government, economics, science, education, cultural aspects, mass media, and religion.

As special research projects and having determined the categories, literally hundreds of items were suggested by the graduate students. The criteria for selecting items included: 1) that they be intrinsically related to the categories; 2) that they would not invade the privacy of the individual; 3) that they would not be offensive; and, 4) that they would hopefully produce a difference on a simple five-point scale, with a minimum of ambiguity.

The weights and number of items for each category were also arbitrary; but these factors were related to the decision of having no more than seventy items. Priority was given to the category of cultural aspects while holding, fairly constant, the items in the other categories. The distribution of these weights and items, also referred to as constructs or objectives transferred to the item form, was as follows:

Categories	Number of Items	Weights
1.1 Government	11	.16
2.2 Economics	10	.14

3.3 Science	6	.09
4.4 Education	8	.11
5.5 Cultural Aspects	17	.24
6.6 Mass Media	9	.13
7.7 Religion	9	.13
Totals:	70	1.00

Since a panel of experts from the various social science disciplines had selected items appropriate to their field, the constructs reflected a wide range of phenomenological aspects regarding the American Way of Life. Most important, after thirteen years of use, the items were still relevant! Understandably, because of its global nature, the category of cultural aspects presented a minor problem of some overlap into other categories. Yet, this overlap was more than compensated by the deeper dimension which the latter category gave to an inquiry of the American Way of Life.

– Reliability

In order to assess the congruency and reliability of the questionnaire, a total of 148 undergraduate students, representing various colleges at St. Cloud State University, were tested during the spring quarter of 1976—approximately thirteen years after the formulation of the items!

– An Index of Congruency

Since the theoretical framework stressed the construct of congruency or relatedness, it seemed reasonable to gain an index of relatedness by determining how consistent items were between pre- and post-tests. Hence, the questionnaire, separated by the beginning and the ending of the quarter, was administered twice to the same population. The index of consistency is presented as follows:

Source	N	Items that were significantly different (via multiple t tests)	Consistency Index
3.1 College of Industry	20	3	.96
3.2 College of Liberal Arts	22	2	.97
3.3 College of Education			
3.31 Human Relations	5	1	.99
3.32 Secondary Education Majors	25	0	1.00
3.33 Elementary Education Majors	76	3	.96
Totals:	148		

– <u>Coefficients of Stability</u>

Finally, in order to establish measures of <u>stability</u> between the pre- and post-test scores, Spearman-Brown correlation coefficients were obtained. As shown below, these coefficients of stability ranged from +.33 to +.85.

Source	N	F	2-Tailed Probability
4.1 College of Industry	20	.81	.001

4.2 College of Liberal Arts	22	.67	.003
4.3 College of Education			
4.31 Human Relations	5	.33	Not Significant
4.32 Secondary Education Majors	25	.85	.001
4.33 Elementary Education Majors	76	.57	.001
Total:	148	.63	.001

– Implications of the Findings

The implications of this study may be summarized as follows: the results pertaining to agreement or disagreement of the various dimensions was provided as:

1. A basis for the development of a citizenship for curriculum.

2. A "treatment" model for value clarification in the content area of the social sciences.

3. Base-line data for future assessment of students, parents, consumers, or other citizens.

4. A greater awareness within the leadership element in American society of some of the issues that divide its people as well as those that unite them, thus affirming or denying the existence of "common core 'values'."

5. An adequate, comparative analysis for those individuals and institutions participating in the study.

＊＊＊＊＊＊＊＊＊＊

The results generated from the thirty samples yielded a tremendous amount of data, and the statistical analysis required over 1200 computer sheets. These data obtained were amenable to two kinds of analyses: analysis of means and analysis of variance.

In the first case, comparisons were made in terms of the mean scores of experts versus the lay publics within each category of government, economics, etc. Since t tests were used to test significant differences between the means, this information was also included.

The format utilized to illustrate data reduction involved both general and specific findings. For example, general findings related to:

1. Comparing the yield of significant differences from the fifteen Minnesota samples with the fifteen nationwide samples.

2. Comparing the percent of agreement between experts and lay publics from both statewide and nationwide samples.

3. Ranking of categories that contained items that were significantly different from each set of fifteen samples.

4. Ranking of categories via the yield of significant differences in each category versus the weighted items for each category.

5. Ranking of categories: Minnesota versus nationwide samples.

6. Indicating the yield of significant differences from all thirty samples.

In the case of specific findings, the analysis was directed to the tabulation of frequencies shown within each category. For example, in the category of government and for each item, the extent of disagreement, indecision, or agreement is indicated between experts and lay publics. All other categories, for each set of fifteen samples and a summarization for the thirty samples, is treated in the same manner. This information is shown in Tables 6 to 8.

An interval analysis for the area of indecision was also provided. It enabled one to determine whether a particular response was due to a majority of subjects marking "3" (i.e., the area of indecision), or whether the area of indecision was due to a lack of consensus (i.e., some combination of 1 and/or 2, the area of disagreement versus a combination of 4 and/or 5, the area of agreement). This interval analysis was performed on the total sample, the Minnesota and nationwide samples, and a random sample of junior and senior high school students.

An analysis of variance was also done for the thirty samples of lay publics. Since there were predictor variables of sex, age, occupation, and geographic location, the author was interested in knowing whether any two of the latter factors produced the significant differences noted between the experts and the lay publics. Again, this analysis was cursory in nature, and any depth probe of this variance was really beyond the intent or scope of this study.

* * * * * * * * * *

The analyses and interpretation of data which I will present in this section are specific in nature. The fifteen Minnesota samples are given first; and then they are followed by the fifteen nationwide samples.

– Specific Findings (Analysis of Means); The Minnesota Samples:

An examination of the significant differences between experts and lay publics indicates the following findings for the categories and for each subcluster of items. It should be noted that special attention was focused on what the majority of samples indicated for the particular category being described.

1. Government—

1.1 That for the majority of samples, with the exception of item 2 (i.e., people should have maximum freedom to interpret laws so they seem to be desirable), there was agreement or indecision on the remaining items.

1.2 That there was complete agreement on such matters as people involvement in the process of government, taxation in terms of one's ability to pay, centralization in government, and understanding of the origins of liberty (i.e., item 22); and that 67 percent believed that political parties are a necessity to good government.

1.3 That 93 percent indicated agreement that "good Americans carry out their responsibilities as citizens."

1.4 That 73 percent are undecided regarding the assertion that "citizens are not living up to the sacred dignity of each individual." Considerable indecision was also registered for the items relating to increased crime (item 43 also showed the greatest number of significant differences although 7 of these were within the interval of agreement while 3 were in the area of indecision, 2 of which were in the same interval), to nonvoting, and to the quest for security being related to the rise of big government.

1.5 That 73 percent disagreed with the notion that people should have maximum freedom in interpreting laws.

2. Economics—

2.1 That only 4 items fall within the interval of agreement. These included the farmer's importance to the nation (i.e., 66 percent) with ten significant differences; the number of hours Americans work (i.e., 73 percent) with 11 significant differences; the honest ways of making a fortune (i.e., 93 percent); and advertising is propaganda (i.e., 66 percent).

2.2 That many items were within the range of indecision. Among these were: the purpose of labor unions (i.e., 93 percent); management is anti-labor (i.e., 80 percent); the amount of the national income spent on food (i.e., 80 percent) with 10 significant differences; the role of mass production 9i.e., 73 percent); and selling successfully via national advertising (i.e., 60 percent).

2.3 That there was only 1 item where the majority of samples expressed disagreement. It concerned the idea that money is success (i.e., 60 percent).

3. Science—

3.1 That only 2 items were within the interval of agreement. One included the idea that "American status symbols have been created through improved technology and science" (i.e., 86 percent), with 7 significant differences in the same interval but differing only in strength of response. The other item contained the notion that "research means better living," with a slim majority of agreement (i.e., 53 percent).

3.2 That most of the items in this subcluster fell within the range of indecision. These included improved transportation being equated to better living, with 4 significant differences in the same interval, but differing only in strength of response (i.e., 87 percent); improved things and living through chemistry (i.e., 80 percent); improved technology means better living (i.e., 67 percent); and improved technology means a higher standard of living (i.e., 53 percent).

3.3 That no majority of samples was observed for the interval of disagreement.

4. Education—

4.1 That there were 4 items in the interval of agreement. Included here were ideas dealing with the development of intellectual curiosity and life-long learning (i.e., 100 percent); understanding of the physical world (i.e., 93 percent); supplementing the parental right for the good of the child (i.e., 67 percent); and education providing an awareness of the world community.

4.2 That three items were noted for the interval of indecision. There is doubt regarding the ability of education to meet individual needs and differences, with 4 significant differences in the same interval but differing only in strength of response (i.e., 93 percent); the connection between democracy and supporting diversity in education (i.e., 67 percent); and the understanding and appreciation of American democracy (i.e., 53 percent).

4.3 That only one item was within the rage of disagreement. It concerned the idea that America provides equal education for all children, with 3 significant differences in the same interval but differing only in strength of response (i.e., 80 percent).

5. Cultural Aspects—

5.1 That there were 5 items within the interval of agreement. These involved aspects as: parents desiring their children to be popular, with 7 significant differences, but 6 of these were in the same interval—differing only in strength of response (i.e., 93 percent); the rise of juvenile delinquency (i.e., 67 percent); fads controlling fashion (i.e., 79 percent); the unity of the family in relation to play (i.e., 93 percent); and children reflecting their home environments, with 3 significant differences occurring in the same interval, differing only in strength of response (i.e., 100 percent).

5.2 That 5 items fell in the range of indecision, and these included: the role of the father as provider (i.e., 86 percent); the uniqueness of music in America (i.e., 86 percent); children having too much (i.e., 64 percent); the inability of parents in controlling their children (i.e., 93 percent); and the father handling harsh discipline (i.e., 57 percent).

5.3 That 5 items were in the interval of disagreement. These involved: not reaching a goal by the age of 40 equating failure, with 2 significant differences occurring in the same interval, differing only in the strength of response (i.e., 86 percent); baseball being America's favorite sport (i.e., 60 percent); women marrying at the age of 20, with 5 significant differences, but 4 of these were in the same interval—varying only in strength of response (i.e., 100 percent); America not having any strong traditions, with 2 significant differences (i.e., 93 percent); and a woman's place being in the home (i.e., 86 percent).

5.4 That 2 of the items were evenly divided between the intervals of disagreement and indecision. Included here were: the decision-making role of the father (i.e., 50 percent); and women being married and having children (i.e., 50 percent).

6. Mass Media—

6.1 There were 3 items in the interval of agreement. These included: Americans are avid television watchers (i.e., 100 percent); comics and sports being desired most in the newspaper (i.e., 53 percent); and the indispensability of the telephone (i.e., 93 percent).

6.2 There were 4 items within the range of indecision: first, the popularity in the reading of two magazine periodicals, with 2 significant differences (i.e., 87 percent); second, the influence of television in choosing products (i.e., 60 percent); third, the popularity of situation comedies, with 1 significant difference (i.e., 93 percent); and fourth, the popularity in reading the "gossip" and "advice" column with 11 significant differences (i.e., 93 percent).

6.3 There were only 2 items in the interval of disagreement. Included were: a men's magazine reflecting the virility of young American men (i.e., 73 percent); and television being the best mode of entertainment (i.e., 80 percent).

7. Religion—

7.1 There were 3 items within the area of agreement. These involved the ideas of: religious tolerance in America (i.e., 67 percent); Americans being "Sunday" Christians, with 3 significant differences (i.e., 73 percent); and the importance of "things" versus religious values in America (i.e., 73 percent).

7.2 There were 6 items in the interval of indecision. Included here were the following: Americans observing the Golden Rule, with 6 significant differences (i.e., 60 percent); America's willingness to "live and let live," with 3 significant differences (i.e., 80 percent); the honesty of Americans, with 11 significant differences, but with only 2 in the same interval (i.e., 80 percent); religious occupations having prestige, with 1 significant

Table 6

Significant Differences of Experts versus Lay Publics in Various Categories of the American Way of Life

(15 Minnesota Samples)

Source								
					Categories			
Experts Versus:	N	Govern-ment	Eco-nomics	Science	Educa-tion	Cultural Aspects	Mass Media	Religion
1. Jr. & Sr. High: Central MN	53	2	5	4	2	2	2	4
2. Jr. High: Alexandria	74	1	4	2	2	0	3	6
3. Sr. High: St. Francis	74	2	4	2	4	1	3	5
4. Adults over 25: Central MN	82	1	2	2	2	2	0	2
5. Adults: Equal diversified occupations, age, sex: Central MN	36	0	3	2	0	2	1	2
6. Elementary Ed. Students	76	2	4	5	2	3	1	5
7. Secondary Ed. Students	25	1	3	2	2	3	1	3
8. College of Industry Students	20	1	3	2	2	3	1	3
9. Human Relations Students	6	1	6	4	3	4	1	3

Table 6 (continued)

10. College of Liberal Arts Students	22	0	3	1	3	1	1	4
11. College of Business Students	29	1	3	1	3	2	0	3
12. Adults of New Hope	209	1	3	1	2	1*	2	2
13. Adults of Central MN: Stratified Hospital Personnel	11	0	3	1	0	1	1	2
14. St. Cloud Business Persons	7	2	2	0	2	4	1	2
15. Equal Number of Elem., Jr. High & Sr. High Teachers	12	1	2	0	1	3	1	0
Totals	736	16	50	29	30	32	19	46

In this particular section, an identical treatment to cull the specific findings from the

interval analysis will also be provided for the 15 nationwide samples.

difference (i.e., 93 percent); religious values being essential to a successful democracy, with 7 significant differences (i.e., 67 percent); and the separation of church and state being essential to the American Way of Life, with 5 significant differences (i.e., 67 percent).

7.3 There was no item of disagreement by a majority.

Before proceeding to the specific findings of the 15 Nationwide samples, in Table 7, the reader can observe the significant differences that occurred between experts and the lay publics in the 15 Minnesota samples.

In this particular section, an identical treatment to cull the specific findings from the interval analysis will also be provided for the 15 nationwide samples.

– The Nationwide Samples

1. Government—

1.1 There were 6 items within the interval of agreement, and these included: involvement of people in the process of government (i.e., 100 percent); taxation based on one's ability to pay (i.e., 87 percent); understanding of the origins of liberty (i.e., 100 percent); good Americans carry out their responsibilities as citizens (i.e., 53 percent); centralization of government (i.e., 93 percent); and man's quest for security (i.e., 53 percent);

1.2 There were 4 items in the range of indecision and these involved: political parties being a necessity to good government, with 8 significant differences (i.e., 87 percent; increased crime, with 2 significant differences in the same interval, but differing in strength (i.e., 60 percent); non-voting (i.e., 80 percent); and the assertion that citizens are not living up to the sacred dignity of each individual (i.e., 53 percent).

1.3 There was only one item of disagreement, and it concerned people having maximum freedom interpreting laws (i.e., 87 percent).

2. Economics—

2.1 There were 3 items of agreement which included: the number of hours Americans work (i.e., 73 percent); honest ways of making a fortune (i.e., 87 percent); and advertising is propaganda (i.e., 87 percent).

2.2 The 6 items of indecision involved: the farmer's importance to the nation, with 8 significant differences (i.e., 73 percent); the proportion of the national income spent on food, with 14 significant differences (100 percent); selling successfully via national advertising, with 3 significant differences (i.e., 67 percent); the purpose of labor unions (i.e., 80 percent); management being anti-labor (i.e., 93 percent); and the role of mass production (i.e., 93 percent).

2.3 The one item of disagreement was that money is success (i.e., 67 percent).

3. Science—

3.1 The one item of agreement was that American status symbols have been created through improved technology and science (i.e., 60 percent).

3.2 The 5 items of indecision included: improved technology means better living, with 5 significant differences (i.e., 67 percent); research means better living, with 6 significant differences (i.e., 53 percent); improved transportation being equated to better living, with 5 significant differences (i.e., 93 percent); improved things and living through chemistry, with only 1 significant difference, but in the same interval (i.e., 93 percent); and improved technology means better living, with 7 significant differences (i.e., 67 percent).

4. Education—

4.1 The sole item of agreement concerned the development of intellectual curiosity and life-long learning (i.e., 87 percent).

4.2 The items of indecision were: understanding of the physical world, with 6 significant differences (i.e., 60 percent); supplementing the parental right for the good of the child, with 3 significant differences (i.e., 85 percent); the connection between democracy and supporting diversity in education, with 6 significant differences (i.e., 67 percent); the ability of education to meet individual needs and differences, with 9 significant differences in the same interval, but differing in strength of response (i.e., 80 percent); understanding and appreciation of American democracy, with 10 significant differences (i.e., 73 percent); and an awareness of the world community, with 3 significant differences (i.e., 67 percent).

4.3 The only item of disagreement was that America provides equal education for all children, with 4 significant differences within the same interval, differing only in strength of response (i.e., 93 percent).

5. Cultural Aspects—

5.1 The 5 items of agreement involved: parents desiring their children to be popular, with 8 significant differences in the same interval, differing only in strength of response (i.e., 100 percent); the rise of juvenile delinquency (i.e., 87 percent); fads controlling fashion (i.e., 80 percent); the unity of the family in relation to play (i.e., 60 percent); and children reflecting their home environments, with

1 significant difference, differing only in strength of response (i.e., 100 percent).

5.2 The 4 items of indecision were: the role of the father as provider (i.e., 73 percent); the uniqueness of music in America (i.e., 93 percent); children having too much (i.e., 93 percent); and the inability of parents in controlling their children, with 1 significant difference (i.e., 100 percent).

5.3 The 8 items of disagreement included: not reaching a goal by the age of 40 equating failure, with 2 significant differences in the same interval, differing only in strength of response (i.e., 93 percent); the decision-making role of the father (i.e., 87 percent); baseball being America's sport (i.e., 60 percent); women marrying at the age of 20, with 6 significant differences within the same interval, differing only in strength of response (i.e., 100 percent); America not having any strong traditions, with 2 significant differences (i.e., 80 percent); women being married and having children (i.e., 87 percent); a woman's place being in the home, with 2 significant differences in the same interval, differing only in strength of response (i.e., 100 percent); and the father handling harsh discipline, with 1 significant difference in the same interval, differing only in strength of response (i.e., 60 percent).

6. Mass Media—

6.1 The three items of agreement included: Americans are avid television watchers (i.e., 100 percent); the influence of television in choosing products (i.e., 60 percent); and the indispensability of the telephone (i.e., 100 percent).

6.2 The 4 items of indecision were: the popularity in the reading of magazine periodicals, with 3 significant differences (i.e., 87 percent); the popularity of situation comedies (i.e., 67 percent); comics and sports being desired most in the newspaper (i.e., 53 percent); and the popularity in reading the "gossip" and "advice" column, with 12 significant differences (i.e., 87 percent).

6.3 The 2 items of disagreement involved: a men's magazine reflecting the virility of young American men (i.e., 87 percent); and television being the best mode of entertainment, with 1 significant difference in the same interval, differing only in the strength of response (i.e., 93 percent).

7. Religion—

7.1 The 2 items of agreement were: Americans being Sunday Christians, with 1 significant difference (i.e., 73 percent); and "things" versus religious values in America (i.e., 87 percent).

7.2 The 6 items of indecision included: religious tolerance in America (i.e., 53 percent); America's willingness to "live and let live," with 1 significant difference (i.e., 93 percent); the honesty of Americans, with 12 significant differences (i.e., 93 percent); religious occupations having prestige (i.e., 100 percent); religious values being essential to a successful democracy, with 10 significant differences (i.e., 87 percent); and the separation of church and state being essential to the American Way of Life, with 4 significant differences (i.e., 60 percent).

7.3 The only item of disagreement was that Americans observe the Golden Rule, with 1 significant difference (i.e., 87 percent).

An analysis and interpretation of these specific findings derived from the thirty American publics—fifteen from Minnesota and

fifteen from the nationwide samples surveyed in this research—
is considered next.

* * * * * * * * *

Both the analyses of means and variance yielded vital
information and knowledge concerning the American Way of
Life. Accordingly, my interpretation is provided in the pages
that follow.

1. Apparently, the 30 American publics surveyed in this
   study had a remarkable congruency of opinions with the
   designated experts. The total agreement of 82.9 percent
   was only slightly higher than the agreement observed for
   both the Minnesota and Nationwide samples. Indeed, the
   homogeneity of the latter two is reflected in an identical
   average for each respective set of samples of 78.5 percent!

2. Neither the number of experts for each category, nor the
   numbers with each sample of the public seemed to affect
   the nature of agreement. The most salient fact in respect to
   the latter is that the 88 experts versus the 1439 individuals
   sampled produced an agreement of 82.9 percent!

3. Geographic location did not seem to be a significant factor in
   the agreement of items between experts and the lay publics.
   For example, the agreement between a lay public in district
   California and experts was 81.4 percent. Conversely, the
   agreement between a lay public in St. Cloud and experts
   was only 68.6 percent, the lowest observed agreement of
   any of the 30 samples!

4. Generally, in comparing the responses made to the 70-
   item questionnaire by the various lay publics, on the 1 to 5
   scale, the interval of 3 or area of indecision was dominant
   in 41 percent of the items for the Minnesota samples and
   in 50 percent of the items for the Nationwide samples.

However, one should not erroneously infer that the indecision was a result of all individuals marking interval three. Hence, it can be concluded that the indecision was a lack of consensus, greater in the Nationwide samples than in the Minnesota samples.

5. The observed significant differences for the seven categories were more evenly distributed in the Nationwide samples than the Minnesota samples. For example, in the former, there was an approximate difference of 2 to 1 between Economics (i.e., ranked first) and Government (i.e., ranked last). While the rankings were identical for the Minnesota samples, the difference between first and last was 3 to 1. Yet, the sheer number of differences between the two sets was almost identical: 226 versus 222! It was quite clear that, depending on the concerns or problems within a particular geographic region, a differential emphasis is placed on education, science, religion, and cultural aspects. Of course, this differential emphasis is also related to certain key items in the categories, and this aspect will be considered below.

6. In view of the congruency or strong relationship between the opinions of experts and lay publics, one must explore differences within the groups, such as characteristics. Both gender and age emerged as significant variables, with age cutting through the majority of categories.

The factor of gender showed significant differences in the subcluster of items related to cultural aspects and religion. While the differences—also with age—were often within the same area of agreement or disagreement, there was more agreement in both categories, among the males than the females about particular items.

7. There were key items within the categories that deserve special elaboration. These are given for each category:

7.1 Government:

While the Minnesota Samples were in agreement with the political experts regarding the necessity of having political parties, this fact was not apparent with the Nationwide samples. One notes a lack of consensus for this item(i.e., 29 percent in interval 3).

There were also 7 Nationwide samples that expressed a lack of consensus for good Americans being those who actively carry out their responsibilities as citizens (i.e., 19.5 percent in interval 3). One senses a basic contradiction between the latter indecision and the 100 percent agreement expressed in the item stating that government should be of the people, by the people, for the people! The political mood of many Americans has been one of cynicism, of distrust in the political process, and a sense of helplessness in a mass society.

There is also considerable doubt regarding the role of the federal government in respect to crime. Those samples that were from or near large population centers tend to agree with the idea that the federal government should help to fight crime. On the other hand, the more distant the setting was from these crime areas, the less the consensus.

7.2 Economics:

Three major concepts were contained in this category—the farmer, food, and work.

As one would suspect, the Minnesota samples agree about the farmer being important to the nation. Conversely, the Nationwide samples lack consensus regarding the importance of his role. The points of tension that exist between farmers and lay publics may be due to the modern methods of packaging, distributing, and selling the farmer's products. For example, how many Americans really understand this complex, impersonal process?

There is a lack of consensus regarding the amount of money spent on food. Americans have been accustomed to an abundance of food at fairly reasonable prices. However, there are ominous signs that the aforesaid abundance may be a thing of the past. Land use has become a critical issue in many parts of the country. Living space versus farming space is a serious problem and it requires thoughtful planning so that one does not suffer at the expense of the other.

The lay publics expressed an agreement regarding the amount of time people work. However, they lacked consensus regarding the purpose of labor unions, especially in their relationship to the working man. It is a tragic circumstance that so many Americans, being on fixed incomes, constantly lag behind in salaries; and that they are caught in a vicious vortex of spiraling prices.

There was no agreement to the assertion that management is anti-labor. Apparently, some lay publics have gained an insight or understanding into the many problems facing management, especially the small businessman who fights for his survival in the marketplace.

More disagreements with experts were expressed by the thirty samples in this category than all others.

7.3 Science:

Generally, the lay publics lack consensus regarding the purposes and roles of American technology. Ironically, in retrospect, it is within this domain that the Americans have excelled. If the British were characterized by "the sun never sets on the Union Jack," the Americans were known around the world for their "Yankee ingenuity."

Therefore, in view of the doubt expressed by many lay publics, particularly younger people, there appears to be a shifting away from the values inherent in technology. Undoubtedly, the effects of pollution and the current energy crisis have had their influence on the opinions of Americans.

7.4 Education:

Regional differences are apparent in the responses made to this category. For example, the nationwide samples lacked consensus in all but two items, whereas the Minnesota samples indicated more agreement on these items.

However, the crucial issues in this subcluster centered on the idea of diversity. In one case involving whether equal educational opportunity is provided for all children, 26 of the samples disagreed with this assertion. When this item is coupled with another regarding the connection between democracy and supporting diversity in education, a dichotomy is evident. In terms of the latter item, only 9 samples of the 30 could agree!

The factor of age was reflected in this doubt about faith in democracy equating diversity in education. It is most pronounced on the junior and senior high level which had the highest percent for interval 3 in this item.

Since diversity is a factor associated with change, it would seem that more attention needs to be focused on this area. Nevertheless, after seeing the responses made by the three panels of experts in education, they all disagreed on America providing equal education opportunity, but they also all agreed regarding the need for diversity in education as a condition for having democracy. Herein is an excellent example of the split between the morals (in this instance, extolled by experts), versus the mores (as viewed from the opinions of the publics).

It seems that most Americans are suspicious or fear diversity in education and this issue remains a serious source of conflict or confrontation.

7.5 Cultural Aspects:

There was considerable similarity on the items between the Minnesota and Nationwide samples. Two exceptions deserve comment.

First, the majority of Nationwide samples disagreed regarding women marrying and having children; the Minnesota samples were evenly divided between disagreement and indecision.

Second, the majority of Nationwide samples disagreed on a father handling the harsh discipline, while the majority of Minnesota samples lacked consensus on this item.

Since the above items concern important roles in the family, one may infer that the changes have been more pronounced elsewhere than in Minnesota. Age is a significant variable in that, the younger the person, the greater the disagreement toward these two items.

The opinions held about other items, whether agreement or disagreement, show that the impact from the feminist or equal rights movement has had a profound effect on many Americans especially the role of the father and mother in a family situation.

It is interesting to note that an identical number from both the Nationwide and Minnesota samples disagreed that baseball is America's favorite sport. In a very indirect, subtle way, the opinions held toward this spectator sport, a leisure time activity, reflect the more urban taste of twentieth century America. Baseball can be regarded as more pastoral, slower, with each player on the team assigned to a rather extensive area "to cover." In contrast, football, a much faster body-contact sport, has emerged as the sport of the masses.

7.6 Mass Media:

There was considerable similarity between the two sets of samples, although the Nationwide samples agreed to the notion that advertising was the media criteria used by Americans in choosing products; the Minnesotans lacked consensus on this item.

Both the Nationwide and Minnesota samples were unanimous in their agreement relating to Americans being avid television watchers. They are also almost unanimous in their disagreement that television is the best mode of entertainment.

What appears, at first glance, to be a contradiction may be another way of expressing what these articulate publics really feel. In effect, they may be saying, "We don't like what we watch, but how much choice do we have in the selection of what we see?"

Judging from the lack of consensus shown by all 30 samples, Americans may do far more serious reading than is commonly supposed. The popularity of the "gossip" and "advice" column suggests that   many

Table 7

Significant Differences of Experts versus Lay Publics in Various
Categories of the American Way of Life

(15 Nationwide Samples)

Source		Categories						
Experts Versus:	N	Govern-ment	Eco-nomics	Science	Educa-tion	Cultural Aspects	Mass Media	Religion
16. University of Wisconsin, Superior	48	2	3	2	2	1	1	2
17. North Dakota State Univ.	41	0	3	4	2	2	1	3
18. Drake University	47	1	3	1	6	2	1	2
19. Jr. & Sr. High Students of Royal Oak	74	2	4	3	3	0	1	2
20. Cleveland State University	37	2	2	5	2	3	1	3
21. Allegheny College	50	1	2	5	5	1	2	3
22. Edinboro State College	47	1	4	4	4	3	1	3
23. Gannon College	25	1	3	0	2	2	1	1
24. Southern Conn. State College	83	1	4	1	4	5	1	2
25. Florida International Univ.	49	1	3	1	3	0	2	2
26. Sr. High of Merritt Island, Florida	1	3	5	2	3	0	3	3
27. Adults of Charlotte, NC	3	1	3	1	2	3	1	1
28. Adults of Salem, Oregon	1	1	3	7	2	1	1	2
29. Pharmaceutical Employees of San Diego Veteran's Assn.	1	1	2	1	1	1	2	1
30. University of Vermont, Burlington	2	2	1	3	1	3	1	2
Totals	736	20	45	37	45	27	20	32

members of American society find or seek this vehicle of communication as a way of satisfying some inner need, a way of gaining identity, or a way of relieving loneliness, fear, or anxiety.

7.7 Religion:

In comparing the opinions of both sets of publics, the Nationwide samples disagreed about Americans observing the Golden Rule, whereas Minnesotans lacked consensus. However, in both sets, there was a lack of consensus regarding the honesty of most Americans; nearly all samples exhibited significant differences with the experts.

Again, age pervades these items: the younger the individual, the greater the lack of consensus.

While it is difficult to generalize about a given group or people, one senses that, when it involves morality or religion, many Americans are loath to express their true feelings. Hence, they may resort to more neutral opinions, often shading what they really believe.

Finally, similar to the information gleaned from Table 6 from the fifteen Minnesota samples, Table 7 summarizes the significant differences contrasting the experts versus lay publics in the fifteen Nationwide samples.

Most significant, these data revealed a surprisingly high agreement between lay publics—a total of 30—and the groups designated as experts. This congruency, expressed as opinions, gives credibility to the existence of common core values. While there were regional differences, these differences were probably due to the interests or problems unique to that area.

Apparently, as indicated in the various state and nationwide samples, the factors of sex and age proved to be significant, but age produced more differences in six of the seven categories.

Of the significant differences noted in Table 7, the categories of Education and Economics were tied with forty-five apiece; followed by Science, thirty seven; Religion, thirty-two; Cultural Aspects, twenty-seven; and Government and Mass Media with twenty each.

Table 8

Percent of Agreement Between Experts and Lay Publics
Among 30 Samples

Minnesota (N – 736)	Agree-ment	Nationwide (N = 736)	Agree-ment
1. Jr. & Sr. High: Central Minnesota	71.4	1. University of Wisconsin, Superior	81.4
2. Jr. High: Alexandria	74.3	2. North Dakota State Univ.	78.6
3. Sr. High: St. Francis	70.0	3. Drake University	77.1
4. Adults over 25: Central Minnesota	84.3	4. Jr. & Sr. High Students of Royal Oak	78.6
5. Adults: Equal Age, Sex: Central Minnesota	85.7	5. Cleveland State Univ.	74.3
6. College of Ed., El., SCSU	68.6	6. Allegheny College	72.9
7. College of Ed., Sec, SCSU	78.6	7. Edinboro State College	71.4
8. College of Ed., Human Rel., SCSU	68.6	8. Gannon College	85.7
9. College of Ind., SCSU	78.6	9. Southern Connecticut State College	74.3
10. College of Liberal Arts, SCSU	81.4	10. Florida International University	82.9
11. College of Business, SCSU	81.4	11. Sr. High Students of Merritt Is., FL	72.9
12. Adults of New Hope	79.3	12. Adults of Charlotte, NC	82.8
13. Adults of Central MN (Hospital Personnel)	85.7	13. Adults of Salem, Oregon	80.0
14. Business Persons, St. Cloud		14. Pharmaceutical Employees of San Diego	87.1
15. Equal Numbers of El., Jr. & Sr. High Teachers of Northeastern MN	81.4	15. University of Vermont	77.1
	88.6		
Average Percent =	78.5	Average Percent =	78.5
Range:		Range:	
Minimum =	68.6	Minimum =	71.4
Maximum =	88.6	Maximum =	87.1

However, as Table 8 indicates, in comparing the general agreement between experts and lay publics among the thirty samples, the finding was utterly amazing! Imagine, in contrasting opinions between those expressed by the fifteen Minnesota samples versus the Nationwide samples, for 736 persons in each case, the percent of agreement was 78.5! One may conclude that with this high agreement, whatever diversity of opinions that exists among these thirty groups is, at once, a strength, and much less of a weakness. Nevertheless, at present and in the years ahead, a more thorough understanding of diversity may be one of the catalytic agents for change. Assuredly, it can help to bridge the gap between our morals and mores—the "should be" and "what is," respectively. Therefore, the choices we make now and in the future concerning the aforesaid categories will be extremely important to our American Way of Life.

In replicating the same questionnaire utilized for the thirty United States locations, during 1982, I received a research grant from St. Cloud State University to conduct a limited study in Europe. From previous research (i.e., during 1973-74) in several countries there, I selected Germany and Spain. Having made contacts with several individuals in these two countries, the research began during September of 1982.

Fortunately, in my preparation for doing this sampling in Germany and Spain, my friends in these two countries offered to assist me by locating and administering both German and Spanish translations of the American Way of Life (i.e., AWOL). Their combined efforts resulted in locating 79 persons from each country who agreed to participate in my project. For example, they found volunteers in various western German cities, from Neumünster to Herford (i.e., in Westphalia) to Frankfurt. Then, my friend in Spain located his samples mainly from the Madrid metropolitan area and from the more rural areas near Castlelleón de la plana, not far from Barcelona.

Table 9

A Questionnaire Relating to the "American Way of Life"

Please indicate below how you feel about the statements listed on the left. Circle the number of the scale which corresponds to your feeling: 1 is Strongly Disagree; 2 is Disagree; 3 is Undecided; 4 is Agree; or 5 is Strongly Agree.

	SD	D	U	A	SA
1. People should run the government.	1	2	3	4	5
2. Freedom to interpret laws is necessary.	1	2	3	4	5
3. The farmer is the backbone of our nation.	1	2	3	4	5
4. Education is lifelong learning.	1	2	3	4	5
5. Father is the provider in the home.	1	2	3	4	5
6. Parents want their children to be popular.	1	2	3	4	5
7. Our citizens are avid television watchers.	1	2	3	4	5
8. Good government requires political parties.	1	2	3	4	5
9. People work a forty hour week.	1	2	3	4	5
10. Improved technology means better living.	1	2	3	4	5
11. Understanding the physical world is an educational aim.	1	2	3	4	5
12. Unrealized goals by age 40 signifies failure.	1	2	3	4	5
13. Final family decisions rest with father.	1	2	3	4	5
14. Our country has religious tolerance.	1	2	3	4	5
15. Taxation should equate ability to pay.	1	2	3	4	5
16. Food requires a high percentage of our budget.	1	2	3	4	5
17. Research means better living.	1	2	3	4	5
18. Educators supplement parental rights.	1	2	3	4	5
19. Juvenile delinquency is on the rise.	1	2	3	4	5
20. Magazines and periodicals are most widely read	1	2	3	4	5
21. Our citizens observe the golden rule.	1	2	3	4	5
22. Constitutional law equals liberty.	1	2	3	4	5
23. National advertising assures successful selling.	1	2	3	4	5
24. Improved transportation means better living.	1	2	3	4	5
25. Our country provides equal education for all.	1	2	3	4	5
26. Fads control fashion.	1	2	3	4	5
27. Girly magazines reflect male virility.	1	2	3	4	5
28. Our philosophy is the "live and let live."	1	2	3	4	5
29. Our people are responsible citizens.	1	2	3	4	5
30. Fortunes can still be made honestly.	1	2	3	4	5
31. Sophisticated technology creates status symbols.	1	2	3	4	5
32. Faith in democracy implies diversity in education.	1	2	3	4	5
33. America is unique in its music.	1	2	3	4	5
34. *Table 9 (continued)*					5
35. Most of our citizens are basically honest.	1	2	3	4	5
36. A strong central government lessens freedom.	1	2	3	4	5
37. Advertising is propaganda.	1	2	3	4	5

Table 9 (continued)

38. Chemistry assures better things.	1	2	3	4	5
39. Baseball/soccer is our favorite sport.	1	2	3	4	5
40. Women should marry by age 20.	1	2	3	4	5
41. Comedies are the favorite programs on TV.	1	2	3	4	5
42. Religious occupations hold prestige.	1	2	3	4	5
43. Increased crime makes necessary more government involvement.	1	2	3	4	5
44. Money is success.	1	2	3	4	5
45. Technology means a higher standard of living.	1	2	3	4	5
46. Our country has no really strong traditions.	1	2	3	4	5
47. Children of today have too much.	1	2	3	4	5
48. Comics and sports are most widely read.	1	2	3	4	5
49. Most of our citizens are Sunday Christians.	1	2	3	4	5
50. Non-voting is due to apathy.	1	2	3	4	5
51. Labor unions benefit the working man.	1	2	3	4	5
52. Education recognizes individual differences.	1	2	3	4	5
53. Women should be married and have children.	1	2	3	4	5
54. Parents fail to control their children.	1	2	3	4	5
55. The "advice" column is most widely read.	1	2	3	4	5
56. Religious values are essential to democracy.	1	2	3	4	5
57. Our security is responsible for big government.	1	2	3	4	5
58. Management is anti-labor.	1	2	3	4	5
59. Education enables students in understanding democracy.	1	2	3	4	5
60. A woman's place is in the home.	1	2	3	4	5
61. A family that plays together stays together.	1	2	3	4	5
62. The telephone is indispensable.	1	2	3	4	5
63. "Things" are more important than religious values.	1	2	3	4	5
64. Citizens fail to stress individuality.	1	2	3	4	5
65. Everything is made on mass production.	1	2	3	4	5
66. Education develops student awareness of world relations.	1	2	3	4	5
67. Father should handle the harsh discipline.	1	2	3	4	5
68. Children reflect the home environment.	1	2	3	4	5
69. Television is the best mode of entertainment.	1	2	3	4	5
70. Separation of church and state is essential.	1	2	3	4	5

Concurrent with their efforts during September and October of 1983, I interviewed ten German and two Spanish leaders from the same aforesaid geographic areas. The results from these interviews are summarized in a later section.

Upon my return to Minnesota, the 79 questionnaires that were obtained from each of the aforesaid countries were analyzed, compared, and then correlated with the 1,420 validated U.S. nationwide samples. Following an intensive and thorough computer analysis done at S.C.S.U. of the data obtained from both Germany and Spain, the findings were most encouraging and gratifying. For example, it was discovered that 25 items extracted from the 70 items shown in Table 9 which depicts my questionnaire relating to the "American Way of Life," were concurrent with 30 nationwide sampling.

With the above background and information provided for the general research plan, the following section involved these analyses and summary: 1) the analysis of findings from Germany, Spain, and the United States; and 2) generalizations or relationships gleaned from the findings of the 79 persons sampled in both countries including a summary and analysis of statements made by the 12 leaders from the above countries in the areas of science, business, education, and transportation.

These findings and analyses are the substance for Appendix B.

Appendix B:

The European Samples

— Analysis of the European Samples as Compared
to the 30 Nationwide Samples in the United States

First, when the 79 German and Spanish samples (i.e., N = 158) were compared to the nationwide samples done in the U.S. for a total of 1630, the index of congruency or consistency of responses varied with the seven categories comprising the 70 item questionnaire. The congruency of responses was defined as the consistency of "Agreement, Undecided, and Disagreement" for each item. In other words, for item 1, "People should run the government," the mean score for that question was in the interval of Agreement for all three countries. The same procedure was employed for determining the congruency of "Undecided" and "Disagreement" for Items 54—"Parents fail to control their children"—and 60—"A woman's place is in the home"—respectively. Most important, in the matter of interpretation for both the 30 American samples of AWOL and the replicated European research, the Likert five-point scale was utilized. This useful scale ranged from Strongly Agree, 3.50 to 5.00; Undecided, 2.50 to 3.49; and Strongly Disagree, 1.00 to 2.49.

Second, via a computer analysis of the European, responses from Germany and Spain were compared to the 30 American samples to determine an index of consistency or congruency of 25 items from questionnaire shown in Table 10.

Third, surprisingly, with the one exception of science, which revealed that there was <u>no congruency</u> of responses for the six items in this particular category, there were 25 items that <u>were</u> congruent for the remaining six categories. In Table 11, an "Index of Consistency," the reader is provided with a succinct compilation of relevant information.

Fourth, when one considers that the German and Spanish translations were made from the AWOL, the 25/70 or 36 percent of the items that were congruent, this consistency reflected a commonality of feeling toward the values inherent in the items. In view of the lack of congruency in the category of science, for the 25 items, the top ranked category was education and the lowest was science. It begs the question: What precisely were these items that were congruent?

Fifth as depicted in Table 10, the description of each item for the six categories are indicated. Except for the category of government, where there was perfect agreement on all three items, the remaining five categories involved responses that were mixed. For example, in each country, in the category of economics, the responses for three of the four items were undecided. This variance in responses was also typical for the remaining four categories.

Sixth, an inspection of the items in each category from government to religion, indicates the responses that were congruent. For example, the response of agreement occurred three times in government; one time in economics; two times in cultural aspects; and one time each in mass media and religion.

1. To my question of: "Why do you think that there is a gap in what we Americans believe to be the 'should be' (i.e., our

Table 10

The Congruency of Items in Six Categories for the United States,
Germany, and Spain
(N = 1630)

Government		Cultural Aspects	
1. People should run the government.	Agree	12. Unrealized goals by age 40 signifies failure.	Disagree
15. Taxation should equate ability to pay.	Agree	19. Juvenile delinquency is on the rise.	Agree
36. A strong central government lessens freedom.	Agree	40. Women should marry by age 20.	Disagree
		46. Our country has no really strong traditions.	Disagree
		54. Parents fail to control their children.	Undecided
Economics		60. A woman's place is in the home.	Disagree
16. Food requires a high percentage of our budget.	Undecided	61. A family that plays together stays together.	Undecided
37. Advertising is propaganda.	Agree	68. Children reflect the home environment.	Agree
51. Labor unions benefit the working man.	Undecided		
58. Management is anti-labor.	Undecided	**Mass Media**	
Education		7. Our citizens are avid television watchers.	Agree
18. Educators supplement parental rights.	Undecided	20. Magazines and periodicals are most widely read.	Undecided
25. Our country provided equal education for all.	Disagree	69. Television is the best mode of entertainment	Disagree
59. Education enables students in understanding democracy.	Undecided		
66. Education develops student awareness of world relations.	Undecided	**Religion**	
		14. Our country has religious tolerance	Undecided
		21. Our citizens observe the Golden Rule.	Disagree
		63. "Things" are more important than religious values.	Agree

Table 11

Index of Consistency

Rank Order of Categories and Index of Consistency for the U.S.,
Germany and Spain Combined

Categories	Percent	Ratio of Items	
1. Education	50%	4/8	
2. Cultural Aspects	47%	8/17	
3. Economics	40%	4/10	For all 70 Survey Items
4. Religion	33%	3/9	
5. Mass Media	33%	3/9	
6. Government	27%	3/11	
7. Science	0%	0/6	

Total 25/70 or 36%
for all three countries

morals) and what we do (i.e., our mores)," I obtained these responses from leaders in Germany and Spain:

1.1 Almost all of the leaders believed that our ideals and dreams of the plentiful society were out of step with the harsh realities of a new economic competition. For example, the United States and Western Europe, except for very specialized technologies (i.e., computers, medical innovations, etc.) were falling behind countries like Japan, where robot technology and electronics were far more advanced.

1.2 German leaders, from professors to nuclear scientists to plant managers, watched with anxiety the growing political power of the "Green People" (i.e., die greunen Leute), originally composed of environmentalists. This symbol of doubt or uncertainty and active protest is reminiscent of our own student protest movement of the 1960's. However, then, the issues in Germany involved nuclear energy, the "guest workers" from Turkey and elsewhere, and the deployment of missles. The protest of the "Green People" was symbolized by the phrase, "We are not playing the game anymore!" (i.e., Wir spielen nicht mir mit!)

1.3 In another interview in Kessel, Germany with a professor at the University there, I learned—among other interesting facts—that very liberal German youth, were members of the aforesaid organization and sympathized with the Turkish cause. This particular professor had been active teaching Turkish youth the German language. At the time of this writing, during September of 1982, as a cultural aspect, the issue of the Turkish guest worker in terms of assimilating into the German way of life was one of considerable feeling. This German resentment toward the Turks was also related to the unemployment (i.e., arbeitlos) problem. However, this professor viewed the unemployment issue much more in depth than just an economic issue.

For example, he believed that the reluctance of the Turks to learn certain German traits, conventions, and practices related to cultural aspects or acculturation was most unfortunate. Therefore, their subsequent desire to retain their own cultural identity was a most serious problem for the German government. As a prototype of other "guest workers" from Italy, Spain, and Jugoslavia, the Turks found it difficult to cope, interact, and apply their unique skills on a horizontal level with other German people.

This problem was most acute for the Germans. At one time, it was established that the Turkish guest workers represented a total of 1,000,000 strong. The reluctance of the Turkish people to accept German practices was evident in many cities. For example, while in Neumünster, I remember seeing an Islamic Cultural Center, complete with a Turkish flag and other artifacts from their country. Unfortunately, one morning, on an inner-city street of Neumünster, I saw a tragic fist fight between a Turkish youth and a middle-age German man. While neither was seriously hurt because it was quickly broken up by other Germans in the neighborhood, this overt display of hostility indicated a deeper point of tension, of strong feelings or covert prejudices.

While these images of the West were not pleasant for me to view, we in America can learn from these cultural aspects or experiences. In terms of present day America, where we are now confronted with the problems of the illegal aliens from Mexico, we can learn from the professor I described earlier in the great compassion he felt for the Turkish youth with whom he worked.

In retrospect, the German people and their government much to their credit, dealt with the problems of acculturation, particularly with their guest workers, with more compassion and practical ways of coping with these problems than we realize. For example, during the month of October, 1982, the German television network made a wise choice by providing considerable prime viewing time for dialogues. These dialogues were between political leaders and diverse groups especially Turkish people regarding current issues. In one instance, I remember the Turkish girl of perhaps 16 or 17 years of age—apparently the daughter of a guest worker—who responded to a topic dealing with citizenship. With deep emotional feelings she responded, "But Germany is my country!" (i.e., 'Aber Deutschland ist mein Vaterland!").

These issues or polemics were quite common then and they continue in present day Germany. While one cannot generalize about the political or social mood of any European country or geographic area, there are particular strongholds of sentiments, practices, or cultural affinities evident in each. It begs the question: to which Germany are you referring? Is it the conservatism that one finds in some regional areas of Bavaria, Cologne, or in Baden—Würtenburg? Conversely, is it the more liberal thinking that one discovers in the Ruhr district, Essen, Dortmund, Hamburg, Hannover, or Berlin?

In fact, later in this section, I will describe the regional differences in political and socioeconomic sentiments that one experiences in Spain. However, before moving in to the next topic, here are some comparative insights I gained from other locations:

— Since the leaders I interviewed embraced Western ideas of a division of governmental power, which division is not changed without the consent of the other, they cherish the freedom to differ and are willing—although they are not always happy about it—to allow for a considerable diversity of opinion.

— They were greatly concerned with the Western World's use of energy, especially within the U.S. During one interview, for example, I was reminded that the U.S. uses a great proportion of energy for our cultural imperatives of mobility, independence, and freedom. For example, to my question, "Does improved transportation mean better living?" the dominant response centered on this answer: if improved transportation involves our railroad system, then the answer is "yes." Considering this dominant theme, for those who are familiar with the European rail system—it is widely used although there are signs of change—one can depend on fast, efficient travel in Western Europe. However, as I traveled south from Denmark, through Germany, to Switzerland, I observed that all three countries, to a greater or lesser extent, were in debt to their rail systems—the heaviest being Germany where, in 1982, a 2 billion mark debt was reported. Why do these countries allow these debts to exist and grow? Let me suggest the following reasons:

First, it is a <u>visible</u>, public debt for which they can account, regardless of higher energy costs and services.

Second, reflecting their ethical imperative of transportation, they believe that <u>everyone</u> should be afforded the opportunity to travel locally (usually on a 20-minute interval schedule) and to any country in Western Europe (on the hour schedule). Thus, it is very common to see many groups of children and youth of

220

all ages with their backpacks, and, a teacher or leader in charge, going to some place of study or interest. Most important, those without means of transportation, especially the elderly, are able to move efficiently and in comfort from place to place.

If we probe deeper into these ethical imperatives of transportation, we can gain several insights to this unique European view. For example, I traveled to the transportation museum ot Luzern, Switzerland where there is a gigantic, historical collection—complete with rails and ties—of railroad cars, buses, and other modes of transportation from all over Europe and America. Since commuter traffic from the suburbs and adjoining areas to the town center is of great importance, these facts emerged from the European vantage point:

1. Commuters can get to the city trouble free, with no traffic holdups nor parking problems.

2. Throughout the year, independent of weather, traveling by rail is relatively safe, on time, and, with electric propulsion, pollution free.

3. There is attractive shuttle service in all directions, with guaranteed, quick connections.

4. One notes a modern, comfortable rolling stock.

5. There are exclusive traffic lanes as well as reasonable passenger rates for commuters and season ticket holders.

Most important for our consideration, the contrast between our practices of transportation in the American Way in comparison to those in Europe yields these following differences:

— Our ethical imperatives are rooted in the idea of considerable mobility and freedom to move great distances.

— Accordingly, during the Eisenhower administration, enabling legislation was passed to construct the thousands of miles to a national interstate highway system.

— While the states eagerly adopted plans to create this vast network of inter-connecting highways, and because the federal government assumed about 90% of the costs, very few considered the ethical imperative of repair and maintenance, of long-range planning.

— Now, years later, we are paying the penalty for this maximum freedom of mobility because the interstate system has deteriorated very rapidly. For example, not long ago, I drove from Detroit to Toledo on Interstate 75—at one time, a beautiful stretch of divided highway. The great frequency of deep potholes posed frequent hazards for my small car at 65 m.p.h., to say nothing of all drivers around me who were doing at least 70 to 75 and even faster!

— There is also the important difference of the millions of cars—only recently smaller in size—on our local and national highways, giving credibility to the European view that we consume enormous amounts of energy for this privilege.

— Herein, is another crucial difference: this almost Viking spirit for each of us to assume a private debt, of which the collective amount for ownership can only be estimated. Those of us who are able to have this ownership are quite fortunate. Yet, how about the young and the older citizens of our country who, especially in our large urban areas, must depend on public transportation? There are at least 17 U.S. cities, with a population of over 1,000,000 where public transportation is a serious problem for city officials.

In summary, then, from these examples which I have provided relating to transportation, the European investment into their visable, public debt may be a form of <u>productive speculation</u>, while our individualistic approach can evolve into an <u>unproductive</u> speculation— despite our valiant and sincere efforts to repair our highway system—and a national crisis! For so many Americans, transportation has <u>not</u> improved and it does not mean better living! My experiences and research in Spain is the final section of these European samples.

* * * * * * * * * * * * * * * * * *

In terms of my visit to Spain during the autumn of 1982, I received extremely valuable assistance from two inspirational professionals. The first person, as noted in a previous section, Mr. Augusto Cucala, was associated with the University of Castellon. It was he who had arranged to locate and administer the 79 survey forms of a Spanish version of my AWOL questionnaire to a mixture of students, citizens, or other persons in his location.

The second professional was Sister Renee Domeier, a faculty member of the College of St. Benedict College at St. Joseph, MN, located within a short distance of St. Cloud and SCSU. As an instructor of Spanish, she periodically accompanied her students of Spanish to a study center located in the metropolitan area of Madrid. Having directed a Study Center in Fredericia, Denmark for SCSU during 1973-74, I know how rewarding academically and culturally the Spanish center in Madrid would be for this particular class of Professor Domeier.

Before leaving for Europe, I had informed Sister Renee of my plans to visit Augusto so that he could help me in his area and in Barcelona. Accordingly, having informed her previously that my knowledge of Spanish—both speaking and writing—was extremely limited, she still graciously invited me to attend the study center in the short time remaining following my work with Augusto.

Fortunately, having made previous preparations and arrangements for Augusto's random sampling with those 79 Spanish persons, his contribution to my research was superb! Before leaving Castellon, Augusto and I shared some of the responses he obtained from the AWOL.

The following generalizations and relationships are those which Augusto shared with me in contrasting the Spanish responses to AWOL to our own way of life. When his perceptions and interpretations are compared to the responses he obtained from his 79 Spanish samples, they are highly related.

1. In terms of the category of government, Augusto related that, following the death of General Francisco Franco during November, 1975, Prince Juan Carlos, son of the pretender to the Spanish throne succeeded him. In fact, he was crowned as head of state two days after the dictator's death. Juan Carlos had a most difficult road to travel because of the diehard supporters of the past regime. Despite this opposition and the continuing violence committed by the ETA in search of Basque independence, the king was, and continues to be, deeply committed to the democratization of Spain. This transition to democracy was reflected from the 79 samples who agreed that "People should run the government," and "a strong central government lessens freedom."

2. Several changes have occurred in the category of cultural aspects. For example, although there is growing evidence of a larger middle class, vertical mobility is extremely

difficult to achieve for the average working class Spaniard. It is common knowledge that great numbers of workers are dissatisfied with their lot or social position. Encouraged by the more radical political position, these workers want immediate change. In contrast, the more moderate groups recognize that social change is a slow process and they urge patience and understanding.

As in most Western countries, the role of women has changed. They are no longer confined to the home, and, with their new independence and success in employment opportunities, marriage and family life are delayed. According to Augusto, because the Spanish mores are rooted in strong traditions, this change in role for their women was slow in coming.

3. By the early 1970's, what had once been mainly an agrarian economy was transformed into an industrialized, urban, and consumer oriented society of the West. The potential for expansion in Spain was greatly assisted by such factors as foreign investment, by government subsidies, and by low labor costs. This economic growth was evident in geographic areas where industry had been traditionally located. For example, industry flourished in the Madrid region, Valencia, Catalonia, and the Basque Country. Without question, this economic growth transformed Spanish society. What had once—under the old regime—been the cherishing of the rural way of life, became a rural exodus to the cities.

4. With the trend toward urbanization, while education for children had improved, there was disagreement regarding equal education for all Spanish citizens. There was also considerable indecision concerning such educational issues as parental rights; the understanding of democratic

practices; and whether education developed an awareness and understanding of world relations.

Fortunately, when I eventually arrived in Madrid by October 20, 1978, in order to visit with Sister Domeier's Spanish class, via a previous arrangement she had made, it was my privilege to meet Professor Joaquian Fabregat. As a faculty member at the University of Madrid, he had apparently been given permission to help Sister Renee with her small class from St. Benedict College of St. Joseph, MN.

Having learned of my research objectives, especially my interest in higher education in his country, he took me to the University of Madrid for a visit. As my personal guide, we visited the School of Agriculture, a division of their College of Science. Here, I observed that the equipment was old, and that the instructor used the methods of lecture, students recite, and then an examination; but also allowing for interaction from his students. The mission of the university followed the classical version: that the university is a repository of knowledge. Apparently, the agricultural problems that emanate from the aridity of its climate and the hilly or mountainous terrain are constant challenges to the content of the curriculum. For example, with the lack of capital for more modern methods, how can the Spanish farmer bring up much needed water which may exist at very deep levels?

In retrospect, the time I spent with Joaquain Fabregat was one of the highlights of my brief stay in Madrid. During our many hours of sharing ideas, I related some of my experiences during my first visit to southern Spain in early December of 1973. As an American from the mid-size city of St. Cloud, MN, Joaquain asked me to share with him my perceptions and memories of that very first visit. Accordingly, these are the experiences which I related to him:

I was fascinated by the geographic area of Andalucia or Costa del Sol. One was immediately impressed by the number of new buildings along the coast. The towns of Marbella, Funegisola, Torremolinos, and Malaga benefit greatly from the tourist industry—the apparent basis of its economy.

Everywhere, here, as soon as one leaves the main highway, the streets become narrow and winding. Since there are many foothills near the entire coast, as one proceeds northward, the elevation gradually increases. At any moment, one expects Don Quixote and his assistant to come slowly down a nearby mountain trail with his mule and pack.

The Spaniards of Andalucia have, in their features and their mannerisms the physiognomy of their ancestral Arabs who were here for so many generations. The Flamingo music is also vivid testimony of the influences of the Arab people.

The practice of good manners lives on here. For example, while enroute to Marbella, the bus was packed. Yet, whenever a woman boarded, regardless of her age, a male got up to offer his seat to the lady.

In the hotel where I was staying during my short visit, I became acquainted with my waiter, Francisco, and his young apprentice, Manuel, a boy of approximately fourteen years of age. Francisco informed me that he was thirty, single, and has six brothers and sisters all over twenty years of age. He lives with his family at the foothills not far from Torreblanca. His father works with the railroad and the family is quite content with their future on the coast. However, for whatever reason, Francisco disclaims being Andalucian. The only stigma noted thus far was the reputation the people here have for speaking their native Spanish so poorly. I eventually discovered that, for many citizens, they cannot pronounce their "L's" correctly and lisp in the attempt to pronounce some sounds!

Before my departure from Andalucia, I took a guided tour to the historic city of Granada in order to see the beautiful structure, the Alhambra.

Although we left in a heavy downpour of rain, which was the first in eight months, it cleared up within an hour and we had excellent weather thereafter.

Everywhere, along the tortuous winding roads, were scattered houses made of stucco and painted white. Then, nestled in the valley of the mountains, little villages were evident. According to our guide, the chief occupation in Andalucia was farming. He related that here, twenty-seven different kinds of olive trees were cultivated. Everywhere, it seemed, were symmetrical rows of this hardy tree which is extremely capable of withstanding this rather arid climate—really subtropical and similar to southern California.

It was a slow and gradual ascent to the Alhambra, or castle in the sky. One could feel the cold of the Sierra Nevada's as we reached a higher elevation; this particular chain of mountains represents the highest point in all of Spain. As we drew closer to the Alhambra, we saw many caves along the way. Swarms of gypsies inhabit these caves, as have their ancestors for generations past. It was so pathetic to see them, discovering our arrival, rush with castanets and shoe-shine kits to shine our shoes. One girl, no more than twelve, held a little baby, perhaps three months old, and pleaded that her family needed money. Obviously, and it was later confirmed by our guide, she was playing on our sympathy. In fact, we were told that, within, the caves are very clean, comfortable, and have T.V. sets!

How can one describe the beauty of the Alhambra? Washington Irving, upon discovering it in 1829, stayed for two years and ultimately compiled his notes into a book entitled Tales of the Alhambra. His descriptions then were so accurate that they are still appropriate today, although the modern reader might think Irving's treatment as flowery. Nevertheless, when the modern tourist couples his immediate experiences of seeing, hearing, and even touching with the written word, the results are exhilarating. Here, even with the modern conveniences of the asphalt road and a bus, the scene has not changed too radically. In fact, our guide made the interesting insight of the value of <u>time</u> to the Andulacian. He remarked, "You will notice that I do not wear a watch. After all, it is not important; whether I miss my appointment by a half hour does not matter because my client will understand."

And so it is with the Andulacian. Actually, here was the meeting point of two great cultural rivers, two different waters that never touched or fused. The one was old and its current was slowed by the sediments of historical encounters, and, conversely, the other was young, vibrant, and its strong, swift current was suddenly seeking new paths and directions. The mighty Western spirit gained momentum here and began to thrust outwardly with the great explorations of Columbus, and others. Here, from narrow streams, mighty rivers were formed and great waves of historical events washed upon many new lands: witness that after Spain, England, France, Portugal, Holland, and then Germany formed the great Western waves of the future.

One can just imagine a desperate Columbus who, after pleading his case at Granada in 1491 before Ferdinand and Isabella, was about ready to leave, but, at the last instant, Queen Isabella recalled him to relate the good news that his exploration proposal would be granted.

Before my departure from Sister Domeier's Study Center at Madrid, I had a final meeting with Professor Fabregat. Not only did I express my thanks and gratitude to him for the many hours he spent sharing his knowledge and wisdom with me; but I also described the aforesaid events. He listened attentively to my detailed account, smiled, and then explained:

"George, how interesting it is that at Granada, you observed— via the lasting impact that the Arabs made—that, <u>in essence, their culture acted upon Spanish culture</u>." While I agreed with him without any doubt whatsoever regarding the depth and profound implications that he provided, little did I realize how his assertion would remain with me for many years. In fact, it became the catalyst and motivation that later propelled me into several related studies of this cross-cultural phenomenon.

Therefore, in the interaction between two cultures, and, since there are 16 components defined for a culture (i.e., societal, group, personal, morals, etc. as shown in Figure 1), it is crucial to learn <u>which components of one culture produced the differences in the other</u>. For example, in the case of the Arab cultural components impact on the Spanish way of life, the <u>practices</u> of the philosopher Averroes (i.e., Ibn Rushd) was an Arab who was born in Cordova, Spain, and he also lived in the city of Seville. In addition to Averroes' contributions, from the twelfth to the seventieth century, the work of Avecenna (i.e., Ibn Siria) was used throughout Europe as a guide to medical practice. The latter two examples were prototypes of the culturally rich knowledge which was transmitted by the Arabs to the Spanish.

In retrospect, my initial encounter of a "culture acting upon another culture" had been introduced to me while I was a student in the graduate program of Wayne State University—my Alma Mater. Although I only touched on my experiences briefly in the Introduction, as a part-time instructor at Wayne State, I was greatly influenced by one of my former instructors, Dr. Mel Ravitz, professor, <u>par excellence</u>, now retired and former elected member of the Detroit Council City, who inspired me both as his undergraduate and graduate (doctoral candidate) student in his sociology classes. For example, it was he, during this early stage of my career, who introduced me to the ideas of Dr. Leslie A. White, then Professor of Anthropology at the University of Michigan. In his brilliant text entitled <u>The Evolution of Culture</u>, White defines the process of cross-cultural impact as follows:

> *The extrasomatic character of culture is well illustrated by another example: one group acquires culture traits from another. This phenomenon is too well known to require much elucidation. The transfer of culture from one group to another may be occasional and insignificant, or it may take place on a grand scale. It may be fortuitous or deliberately planned and executed.*

However, the importance of Leslie White's insight, and the historical implications that accompanied it, never really came together—not until my visit described above with Sister Domeier's class in Madrid, and my interactions with Professor Fabregat! Then, suddenly, like a journey into my past experiences in the Southwest Pacific Theater of World War II, the light of awareness shined brightly in terms of one culture interacting with another.

For example, I began to recall my experiences as a young soldier while in Papua and New Guinea, from 1942 when I enlisted into the U.S. Army until 1945, a time interval of 31 months overseas, I also endured two more campaigns: the Dutch East Indies and the Philippine Liberation. However, it was in Papua that I witnessed the cross-cultural impact that missionaries from various countries of Europe, the United States, and elsewhere in the world had on the isolated people of Paupua, and the nearby island of New Britain.

Since priests and nuns from Germany, Spain, Holland, and the United States had established the Buna mission in the northern coastal city of Buna, Papua, I saw first- hand the effects of the aforesaid missionaries on the small population at Buna. About 98 percent of this population are Melanesians—a dark-skinned people with black, woolly hair. As soldiers, we were very grateful for their friendship, their gentleness, and their willingness to help us in every way possible. The positive influence of the missionaries on their daily lives and living was apparent to those of us who interacted with them. Since, at the time, they were a protectorate of Australia they volunteered as soldiers in the PIB (i.e., the Papuan Infantry Battalion) in our war against Japan. Then we learned that just a few miles north of Buna in what was known as the "Highlands," there was another group of Papuans who were head hunters and cannibalistic. With such a contrast, it was quite clear that the missionaries, for whatever reasons, had been confined to the geographic region of Buna or elsewhere in New Guinea.

These Papuans of Buna, who lived in elevated huts to escape the mosquitoes, snakes, or other animals, depended on their agricultural skills for growing their own food. With the Japanese conquest of Papua, New Guinea, and other territory in the Southwest Pacific area, survival was difficult for them. Yet, despite the constant danger and challenges confronting them— especially the Japanese destruction of the mission station—they retained the faith, skills, and learning given to them by the missionaries.

In terms of this compassion and willingness to reach out and lend a helping hand, there was a dramatic experience that occurred on the island of New Britain during World War II. For example, it was during 1970—approximately 27 years since my military experiences in Papua and New Guinea—that I attended a professional meeting in St. Cloud; and the after dinner message I heard was simply incredible! The speaker for this particular occasion was Mr. Fred Hargesheimer, at that phase in his life, a sales engineer from White Bear Lake, Minnesota. His fascinating and inspirational experiences are related below.

As a photo reconnaissance pilot for the U.S. Army Air Force, on one of his missions over New Britain, the young First Lieutenant was shot down by a Japanese enemy plane. Fortunately, he ejected safely into the dense, foreboding jungle of the Nakanai ranges on June 5, 1943.

Badly injured, for 31 days alone in the jungle, he evaded the Japanese soldiers who were searching for him. Relying on life-saving techniques he had learned in pilot training, especially how to improvise and adapt to a desperate situation such as he was encountering, Fred managed to survive. For example, he maintained hope by reciting the 23rd Psalm on a daily basis!

Continuing on with his most interesting narration, Fred related how, toward the end of his ordeal, and, ever cautious of the enemy being near, he peered through the dense foliage bordering a well-beaten trail. To his utter amazement, he saw a small group of Nakanai villagers who were singing "Onward Christian Soldiers." Without any doubt whatsoever, Fred recognized this beautiful melody and Christian hymn. Now, with hope and confidence, he quickly positioned himself on the trail, smiled, waved his arms in a friendly fashion to the approaching Nakanai people who had come to rescue him. They, in turn, recognizing that he was the missing American pilot who had been shot down, smiled and brought him back to their village. Apparently, in that dense jungle, these persons from the Nantabee village had paddled up the Pandi river in their canoes in order to reach and rescue Lt. Hargesheimer.

Suffering from the effects of malaria and dysentery, these wonderful people of Nakanai in New Britain, for a period of over 6 months, cared for him and eventually restored his health. Then, as a final gesture of their concern and compassion for Fred, these splendid Nakanai arranged to have a team of Australian Commandos take him under their protection. Eventually, the Commandos arranged to contact the U.S. naval forces in that particular region. Finally, Fred was resuced by the submarine U.S.S. Gato.

It took Fred about an hour to relate this most interesting narrative to an attentive audience. Of course, having been to Papua, New Guinea when I was attached to the 41st Infantry Division of General MacArthur's 6th Army, I wished to share my experiences with him. After his inspiring speech, I introduced myself and before the meeting ended, we spend a half hour discussing our involvement in World War II. My new acquaintance and I, similar to so many others who experienced that painful path to the Philippines, shared similar sentiments. For example, Fred as a pilot and I as a foot soldier, had been exposed to the same fearful challenges which confronted us in the combat zones. These challenges were not only from our enemy, but were also from the constant exposure to the diseases and stress typical of the area—those ranging from malaria to a host of other medical problems. We both concluded that with very few exceptions, there was no other area or region in the world that presented so formidable an obstacle to military operations as did the mountainous and jungle-covered regions of New Guinea as Papua and the nearby island of New Britain.

With further meetings and calls, our friendship blossomed and I learned of Fred's continued association that he maintained faithfully with the Nakanai people. For example, to show his deep gratitude to them for saving his life, during 1963, he returned to New Britain with his son Dick in order to build a school for their children. Today, it is known as the "Arimen's Memorial Primary School" located at Ewasse; and it was the productive result of his discussions with the Rev. Wesley Lutton, the United Church pastor for Central Nakanai at that time. Moreover, his late wife, Dorothy, joined him in Papua, New Guinea for four years as a volunteer at the aforesaid school. By his frequent visits to the Nakanai people for almost 60 years, Fred has renewed ties with the old and new generations as an expression of his love for them.

During 1971, since I was teaching an off-campus class (i.e., for St. Cloud State University) at Maplewood, MN which was not far from White Bear Lake, I invited Fred and his wife to attend one of our evening classes. The course that I was teaching to that particular group concerned curriculum development to this class of approximately 30 teachers who taught at the elementary, middle school, and senior high school levels.

Therefore, as our guests for that evening in October, 1971, and after introducing Fred and his wife to my class, I asked Fred to share his experiences in New Britain as an air force pilot in World War II, and also his plans to return there. After hearing their moving account, and, during a question and answer period, one of the teachers asked me if they could develop curriculum materials for the school that Fred and his wife intended to have built. Of course, this creative project would be extremely helpful for those teachers who would teach in the proposed school. Fred was most grateful when I agreed that this particular project would be a <u>bona fide</u> activity for the class. Then, at a later date, I received a letter from Fred and his wife relating that, with the funds which they had raised and the voluntary labor force, the school had been built, was staffed with teachers, and that it was operating successfully. Most important, they added that the curriculum materials which my class had developed for them were being used successfully.

Reflecting the best sentiments, practices, and traditions of our American Way of Life, this Minnesota couple from White Bear Lake had made the compassionate choice to dedicate their time, energy, and resources in order to make an educational difference to the children of Nakanai! This inspirational project is really a model for all of us!

The latter example provided by a veteran of World War II is a prototype of many, many Americans—both missionaries and ordinary citizens—who, by their volunteer work have made special contributions to enhance the lives of those in other countries. Often, without any fanfare or recognition for their unselfish efforts, these Americans have produced a difference in the lives of those people who received this love and gracious assistance—whatever the form!

Quite clearly, Leslie White's observation about the impact of one culture upon another, can have dramatic consequences, for good or evil. In the examples I have cited from Spain and New Britain, the consequences over time have been helpful or beneficial to those groups or people involved. Conversely, our history books abound with examples of disastrous results from such cross-cultural encounters! Ultimately, the motives underlining the choices made for such interactions as described above are crucial.

The final section of this appendix summarizes the final phase of research begun during 1975 and ending 2006, a span of 32 years—just a few years beyond one generation in time!

Appendix C:

Comparisons of Common Core Values Over Three Time Periods

— An Analysis of the Original, Combined U.S.
and European Samples as Compared to
Two More Recent Samples in the U.S.

Employing the same rationale used for comparing the responses from the 30 U.S. samples, this final section will provide a comparative analysis of two U.S. samples in contrast to the sampling done in the U.S. and Europe during the late seventies. In terms of the locations and time periods, the Regional sample was obtained from Minot and Grand Forks Air Force Bases in North Dakota; from Charlotte, North Carolina; and from Destin, Florida during 1987.

Then, as stated earlier, the second U.S. sample was obtained from St. Cloud State University during May of 2006. Table 12 provides the congruency of responses for the items among the three time periods. It should be noted that a computer analysis of variance (i.e., ANOVA) to determine significant differences was not done because of the small sample sizes (i.e., Regional = 74 and SCSU = 84) in contrast to the U.S. and Europe (i.e., N = 1630). However, the ANOVA was performed within the Regional and SCSU samples, and, surprisingly, very few items

Table 12

The Congruency of Items for the U.S., Germany, and Spain Compared to
Two U.S. Samples: Regional (1987) and SCSU (2006)

N = 1630 U.S., Germany and Spain		N = 76 U.S.: Regional	N = 84 U.S.: SCSU
Government			
1. People should run the government.	Agree	Agree	Agree
15. Taxation should equate ability to pay.	Agree	Agree	Agree
36. A strong central government lessens freedom.	Agree	Agree	Undecided
Economics			
16. Food requires a high percentage of our budget.	Undecided	Undecided	Agree
37. Advertising is propaganda.	Agree	Agree	Agree
51. Labor unions benefit the working man.	Undecided	Undecided	Undecided
58. Management is anti-labor.	Undecided	Undecided	Undecided
Education			
18. Educators supplement parental rights.	Undecided	Undecided	Undecided
25. Our country provides equal education for all.	Disagree	Disagree	Undecided
59. Education enables students in understanding democracy.	Undecided	Undecided	Undecided
66. Education develops student awareness of world relations.	Undecided	Undecided	Agree
Cultural Aspects			
12. Unrealized goals by age 40 signifies failure.	Disagree	Disagree	Disagree
19. Juvenile delinquency is on the rise.	Agree	Undecided	Undecided
40. Women should marry by age 20.	Disagree	Disagree	Disagree
46. Our country has no really strong traditions.	Disagree	Disagree	Disagree
54. Parents fail to control their children.	Undecided	Undecided	Undecided
60. A woman's place is in the home.	Disagree	Disagree	Disagree
61. A family that plays together stays together.	Undecided	Agree	Agree
68. Children reflect the home environment.	Agree	Agree	Agree
Mass Media			
7. Our citizens are avid television watchers.	Agree	Agree	Agree
20. Magazines and periodicals are most widely read.	Undecided	Undecided	Undecided
69. Television is the best mode of entertainment.	Disagree	Disagree	Disagree
Religion			
14. Our country has religious tolerance.	Undecided	Undecided	Undecided
21. Our citizens observe the Golden Rule.	Disagree	Undecided	Undecided
63. "Things" are more important than religious values.	Agree	Disagree	Disagree
The number and percent of items that were congruent or consistent from six categories.		$\frac{22}{25}$ or 88%	$\frac{17}{25}$ or 68% with U.S., Germany and Spain $\frac{18}{25}$ or 72% with Regional

in each of six categories were significantly different in terms of location. These findings and interpretation are presented below.

—The U.S. Regional versus the U.S. and Europe (i.e., N = 1630)

Of the total 25 items, 22 or 88 percent of the Regional responses were congruent with N = 1630. When I compared the pattern of responses (i.e., agree, undecided, or disagree), analysis was made of the pattern of responses (i.e., see Table 12), the following was evident:

- The response of "Agree" occurred on two items in <u>Government</u> regarding "People should run the government," and "Taxation should equate ability to pay"; in <u>Economics</u> for the items "Food requires a high percentage of our budget" (i.e., note the different response of "Undecided" given for the same item by the Regional sample from 1987. Apparently food costs more in the interval of time since then); and that "Advertising is propaganda"; in <u>Education</u>, the one item that "Education develops student awareness of world relations" (i.e., again the response given by the SCSU varies from the "Undecided" provided by the Regional group of 1987. Since then, the emphasis on cross-cultural education demonstrated by SCSU has produced a difference in this item); in <u>Cultural Aspects</u>, there were two items that follow the pattern of the Regional responses—"A family that plays together stays together (i.e., in contrast to the earlier response of N = 1630 indicating "Undecided"); and that "Children reflect the home environment"; and in <u>Mass Media</u>, there was only one item—"Our citizens are avid television watchers." For the three items in <u>Religion</u>, the response of "Agree" was not evident, and for the twenty-five items, there was a total of nine responses for this response in all categories.

- While the response of "Disagree" did not occur within the three categories of Government, Economics, and Education, in Cultural Aspects there were four items that contained this response. These items included "Unrealized goals by age 40 signifies failure"; "Women should marry by age 20"; "Our country has no really strong traditions"; and "A woman's place is in the home"; in Mass Media, "Television is the best mode of entertainment"; and in Religion, "Things are more important than religious values."

- The final comparison involved the response of "Undecided" which occurred eleven times, and these were divided among the six categories. For example, in Government, "A strong central government lessens freedom"; in Economics there were two items, "Labor unions benefit the working man"; and "Management is anti-labor"; in Education there were three items, "Educators supplement parental rights"; "Our country provides equal education for all"; and "Education enables students in understanding democracy"; for Cultural Aspects, Mass Media, and Religion, this response was evident five times: in Cultural Aspects, ""Juvenile delinquency is on the rise"; and "Parents fail to control their children"; in Mass Media, "magazines and periodicals are most widely read"; in Religion, "Our country has religious tolerance"; and "Our citizens observe the Golden Rule."

Since twenty years have elapsed between the Regional and current SCSU sample, and, as Table 12 indicates, there is more congruency between these two samples than between SCSU and N = 1620 (i.e., 68% versus 72%), the comparison between SCSU and the Regional yielded these general findings:

- That for three of the six categories of AWOL, there was absolute or perfect congruency! These included the categories of <u>Cultural Aspects, Mass Media</u>, and <u>Religion</u>.

- That in the category of <u>Education</u>, three of the items were Undecided (i.e., regarding parental rights, equal education, and an understanding of democracy). However, the 84 students at SCSU who participated in the survey noted the growing awareness of world relations which resulted in their agreement with this particular item (i.e., #66). Having directed the very first Study Center in Europe from SCSU during the academic year of 1973-74, I observed the dynamic changes that occurred in these 125 undergraduate students. Their first-hand experiences in Fredericia, Denmark and in other countries which they visited gave them a deeper understanding and appreciation of the vital need for cross-cultural education. Most fortunately, the leadership and faculty at SCSU have been at the forefront in developing and continuing programs in several European countries and elsewhere—especially Japan, which, over the years, at Akita, has participated in sending their students to our university; and, in turn, SCSU reciprocates by sending their students to Akita.

- That for the category of <u>Government</u>, only one item was not congruent and it concerned "A strong central government lessens freedom." The response of Undecided may signify that the shaping forces in America, particularly our continued war with Iraq, are having an impact on opinions regarding our continued involvement.

- That for the category of <u>Economics</u>, except for one item, the other three items were perfectly congruent with the Regional and N = 1630 samples. The item of "Agree" from the SCSU sample stated that "Food requires a high percentage of our budget." Without doubt, in

Table 13

The Distribution of Responses by Categories for Agree,
Disagree and Undecided

- For those responses of "Agree":		
Category	Item No.	Description of Item
Government	1	People should run the government.
	15	Taxation should equate ability to pay.
Economics	37	Advertising is propaganda.
Education		(None)
Cultural Aspects	68	Children reflect the home environment.
Mass Media	7	Our citizens are avid television watchers.
Religion		(None)
(There were 5 items of Agreement.)		
- For those responses of "Disagree":		
Category	Item No.	Description of Item
Government		(None)
Economics		(None)
Education		(None)
Cultural Aspects	12	Unrealized goals by age 40 signifies failure.
	40	Women should marry by 20.
	46	Our country has no really strong traditions.
	60	A woman's place is in the home.
Mass Media	69	Television is the best mode of
Religion		entertainment.
		(None)
(There were 5 items of Disagreement.)		
- For those responses of "Undecided":		
Category	Item No.	Description of Item
Government		(None)
Economics	51	Labor unions benefit the working man.
	58	Management is anti-labor.
Education	18	Educators supplement parental rights.
	59	Education enables students in
		understanding democracy.
Cultural Aspects	54	Parents fail to control their children.
Mass Media	20	Magazines and periodicals are most widely
		read.
Religion	14	Our country has religious tolerance.
(There were 7 items of Indecision.)		

terms of the rising costs and prices in the marketplace concerning many different products and perishable foods, this response reflects the changes taking place in current American society. Those years between 1987 (i.e., the year of the Regional sample and this very year) have witnessed profound changes in the mores, practices, and attitudes of the average American consumer. The production, distribution, and consumption of food remain as vital now and in the future for the appropriate decision maker.

* * * * * * * * * * * * * * * * * * * *

One final step remains to complete these analyses of data from cross-cultural sources. While the reader is encouraged to provide his/her own interpretation for the responses shown in Table 12, a summary table is also provided to indicate those items from all three time settings (i.e., the mid 70's, 1987, and 2006) that resulted in the identical responses for all those sampled. Accordingly, Table 13, followed by my interpretation, will complete Appendix C.

Interpretation

From the sequential sampling of the identified 25 items from the AWOL in two European countries and from various samples throughout the U.S., these generalizations are appropriate:

- That the amazing number of identical responses for six categories totaled $^{17}/_{25}$ or 68%, extending over a time span of over 30 years—slightly more than one generation!

- That the proportional percent of identical items for each type of response such as "Agree, Disagree, or Undecided" was 20% for Agree; 20% for Disagree; and 28% for Undecided.

- That in terms of consensus, a vital factor in a democracy, especially within the category of <u>Government</u>, it was most encouraging to note that two items were rated "Agree" by all three samples. These items concerned people running their government and the belief that taxation should equate one's ability to pay.

- That in consideration of the vital process of attaining consensus, the seven items of Indecision, coupled with the five items of Disagree, are valid reflections of the polemics which permeate the five categories—from <u>Education</u> to <u>Religion</u>.

For example, in the process of acculturation which was defined in the Prologue, the public school becomes a true neighborhood institution. In the continual interaction process between the child-teacher-home, a very important Latin term at one time, defined that trusting relationship. It was "<u>loco parentis</u>," meaning that while in school, the teacher <u>was in place of the parent</u> in guiding the child. Fortunately, in our American Way of Life, hundreds and hundreds of teachers, at all grade levels, still practice that trusting relationship we no longer recognize as "<u>loco parentis</u>." It is this important practice that really defines the substance for the item that "Educators supplement parental rights," which resulted in no agreement as an ethical imperative for the dedicated teacher in America. Despite the continued attacks which lower her/his morale and the active or hidden antagonism by numerous sources, these fine teachers continue to serve their community and school.

Cultural Aspects is another category that reflects the profound changes in our mores and morals. For example, except for three items that involve the family and children, when some measure of Agreement was evident (i.e., particularly in the Regional and SCSU 2006 samples), the other six items were mostly Disagree and Undecided. Here, one finds the dramatic changes that have occurred for women within a single generation. While one item concerned the age that women should marry, the other related to her traditional role in the home.

Most unfortunately, these changes in the role of women have had an enormous impact in terms of social and psychological aspects. Beginning with the feminism movement of the early 1960's and continuing with its advocates today, absence in the home—especially when a family with children are involved—is discouraging. Ironically, while women have made great strides in achieving careers formerly closed to them such as the practice of law or medicine, so many splendid women have <u>not</u> experienced the justice and fairness due them! Without doubt, the significant contributions of women to the American Way of Life have actually strengthened our cultural vitality!

One may ask: why is it that the feminist belief in independence or autonomy passes over lightly or ignores women's historic role of domesticity? Whatever happened to the sentiment that a home is where your <u>husband</u> lives—not just your boyfriend, and where your children live and learn, bound together by the spiritual cement of faith, agape, and philio love? In my own case on a very personal note, coming from a large family of seven children, like the majority of human beings, we found our happiness in a happy home with our father and mother as our models. To be the manager of her home was the main ambition of our dear mother and she attained that goal with joy; from having our house clean; preparing our meals; and washing and ironing our clothes! We children never heard her whine or complain about her role, or the many tasks which she performed. However, she did not shoulder these household tasks <u>alone</u>. Our thoughtful and wonderful father made his contributions— in addition to being fully employed at the time—to the home which, by convention or nature, were <u>his</u> tasks. For example, whenever possible he even helped my mother by cooking meals or assisting her with the household chores. In similar manner, my brothers, sisters, and myself also shared in these tasks—making my mother's basic responsibility of being manager much easier. Thus, this polarity of roles between my parents was a constant inspiration to us and helped us in the choices we made in the years that followed.

* * * * * * * * * * * * * * * * * * *

From this major, longitudinal research effort, the 25 items extracted from the samples done within the U.S. were compared to those done in Europe. This comprehensive analysis yielded a total of 17 items or 68% from the combined AWOL European samples where these responses were absolutely congruent or identical in agreement. I believe that this congruency in itself—discovered in a period of time which extended over 30 years—is incredible!

Finally, in contrasting this important portrait of diversity, it must be remembered that both Germany and Spain have long and different historical patterns, traditions, and their interpretations of the past when they are compared to those in our American Way of Life. However, despite these aspects of diversity, there was a <u>commonality of responses</u> from those Europeans and Americans who were sampled. Therefore, it is quite clear that these 17 identical responses can be characterized as common core values resulting from these analyses.

Considering the accumulation of reliable and valid evidence that was used for creating this book with certain modifications or changes in some of the questionable practices which were described in the Prologue, progress can and must be made to rectify those practices. Most significant, we must bridge or close the gap between the cultural components of Morals (i.e., the "Should be" or "Ideal") and the Mores (i.e., the "Actual" or "Is"). Our citizens of the future—those young children and adolescents presently living in our society—will eventually learn or discover that our loss of cultural vitality is serious to the continuation of our AWOL. Hopefully, their prudent and wise choices will rectify the problems resulting from the atomization of our cultural elements.

Being an educator of many years as a master teacher of all grade levels, administrator, and university professor, I have much confidence in the resistance of our young people—although it could occur more often than it presently does—to the overdose of violence, sex, and other distorting portrayals of normalcy to which they are exposed most frequently on television or other sources. Yet, from my experiences, I have learned that the youthful personality has an amazing resilience and initiative, stimulated in part by the very extreme individualism which we often criticize! In our present-day society, where the maturation process has been accelerated by many factors, our young children and adolescents are far too dynamic to be subdued by the pessimism of the historical movement! Fortunately, they can learn much from the wisdom of General Douglas MacArthur, our great military leader of World War II. In his address to the young cadets at West Point on May 12, 1962, he stated:

> **Duty, honor, and country: these three words reverently dictate what you ought to be, what you can be, what you will be. They are the rallying point to build courage when courage seems to fail; to regain faith when there seems to be little cause for faith; and to create hope when hope becomes forlorn.**

This inspirational message and choice of words, appropriate at all times, can be an image of the future for every American—regardless of geographic location, age, or gender.

* * * * * * * * * * * * * * * * * * *

In my many years of involvement with this research project, I learned considerably in the way of knowledge and information. How fortunate it was that both in our country and in Europe, I was able to share ideas—particularly the background, rationale, and results of my original AWOL project—with professionals in the field who were simply outstanding in their cooperative assistance.

Now that my book is completed, I am hopeful that its contents will give the reader a new and different perspective to such concepts as values, cross-cultural, and the many components of our Western culture. I am also hopeful that my numerous findings and conclusions will lead to a better understanding of our AWOL and cross-cultural values. Perhaps, with increased understanding, another replication could be done employing my rationale or a comparable method. In any event, the contents herein will provide valid, base-line data, knowledge, and information for future years.

Finally, as I explained in my Introduction, this contribution does not resemble the usual format for a book. After the many years I have spent in traveling to many parts of the world, and, after my exhaustive research efforts to compile material from many parts of our country and several locations in Europe, there is one realization that is crystal clear to me and it is this conclusion: with all of our faults, problems, and shortcomings as a nation, there is no better place to live than in America! I am proud to be an American; and I am forever grateful for the opportunities it has offered me to become a contributing citizen!

About the Author

After thirty-one months of overseas service with the U.S. Army during WW II in the Southwest Pacific Theater with General MacArthur George Alexander Farrah received his higher education at Wayne State University, Detroit, Michigan. His doctorate is in the area of research and evaluation, and he has taught at all levels as a master teacher and university professor in Michigan and Minnesota. Dr. Farrah has had a varied career, both in education and in the field of preventative medicine. For example, his professional experiences include positions in teaching—over 40 years in graduate education—and administration.

His five decades in education and preventative medicine included working as a part-time instructor at Wayne State University while being employed as the Director of a Cooperative Teaching Center in Detroit; Consultant for the U.S., Office of Education; Professor and Director of Graduate Field Studies, Center for Educational Leadership and Administration, St. Cloud State University (SCSU); and Director of the Denmark Study Center for SCSU located at Fredericia, Denmark. As the very first program in Europe during the entire academic year of 1973-73, it involved 125 university students and 12 professors from all disciplines on campus.

George's writings, public appearances on programs throughout the U.S., and academic interests reflect the findings of numerous, funded research projects, both in the U.S. and Europe. In fact, the research conducted for this particular book was one of the few reported for the twentieth century that exceeded thirty years of continuous research. Accordingly, during his career, he has received many honors, scholastic and otherwise. For example, in 1971, breaking a one hundred year old tradition at SCSU, the graduating class selected Dr. Farrah to give the commencement address which he did. Another very significant recognition and honor is described below.

It should be noted that Dr. Farrah's intense interest and involvement in the field of preventative medicine, especially nutrition, is not a passing fancy or spur of the moment activity. For example, one of the highlights of his entire career was the research he conducted for the late Linus Pauling, Ph.D., the winner of two unshared Nobel Prizes. While in Europe during 1982, he was working on a funded, cross-cultural research project for SCSU. A Danish doctor in Copenhagen related Pauling's research to him regarding the relationship between collagen and general health—particularly those persons with cancer, and he encouraged him to replicate Pauling's findings because of flaws he had found in the data. Therefore, after returning to the U.S., George replicated the data which has been reported in the National Academy of Science publication. From his own design, Dr. Farrah discovered that his replication revealed a statistical significance that was higher than claimed in the original research. When he notified Dr. Pauling of his findings, the results were reported in the Newsletter, published nationally, by "The Linus Pauling Institute of Science and Medicine." Then, by June of 1999, Oregon State University—Pauling's Alma Mater—invited George to submit his replicated research papers. He complied, and his research and correspondence are now included in Oregon State University's library in the "Ava Helen and Linus Pauling Papers."

Since his retirement from SCSU in 1985, Dr. Farrah continues to be active. First, he accepted an assignment from Central

Michigan University (CMU) as a professor in their Extended Graduate Degree Program at various military bases in the U.S. Not only did he teach research and leadership courses for them; but from 1996 to the present he has reviewed over 2400 Integrated, Graduate Research projects for CMU. Second, he volunteers as the Director of the Center for the Study of Values for Resource, Training, and Solutions; an Educational Service Cooperative in St. Cloud, MN.

Finally, as a member of the American Diabetes Association, he also volunteers at SCSU with the Human Performance Laboratory in order to assess those students who have been diagnosed to be pre-diabetic. The <u>Adherence Inventory</u> which he co-authored has proved to be effective in working with these students.